JAPAN PHOTOBOOK
Shinjuku · Shibuya · Akihabara

By Paul Su

This publication is designed to provide accurate and authoritative information in regard to the subject matter covered. It is sold with the understanding that neither the author nor the publisher is engaged in rendering legal, investment, accounting or other professional services. While the publisher and author have used their best efforts in preparing this book, they make no representations or warranties with respect to the accuracy or completeness of the contents of this book and specifically disclaim any implied warranties of merchantability or fitness for a particular purpose. No warranty may be created or extended by sales representatives or written sales materials. The advice and strategies contained herein may not be suitable for your situation. You should consult with a professional when appropriate. Neither the publisher nor the author shall be liable for any loss of profit or any other commercial damages, including but not limited to special, incidental, consequential, personal, or other damages.

Book Cover by Paul Su
Photos by Paul Su
1st edition 2023

SOCIAL MEDIA SITES (SNS)

YouTube: https://www.youtube.com/c/TokyoPaulLive
Instagram: https://www.instagram.com/tokyopaullive
Twitter: https://twitter.com/tokyopaullive
Facebook:
https://www.facebook.com/groups/tokyopaul (groups)
https://www.facebook.com/TheTokyoPaul (page)

ACKNOWLEDGEMENTS

I want to convey my sincere appreciation to the viewers of my YouTube channel Tokyo Paul, who gave me support and motivation when I was working on this project. This book would not have been possible without their support.

I also like to express my gratitude to my wife for her help. Her invaluable feedback and support were essential in making this idea a success.

I want to thank my family, friends, and readers again for their kindness and support. Thank you to everyone from the bottom of my heart.

SHINJUKU STATION

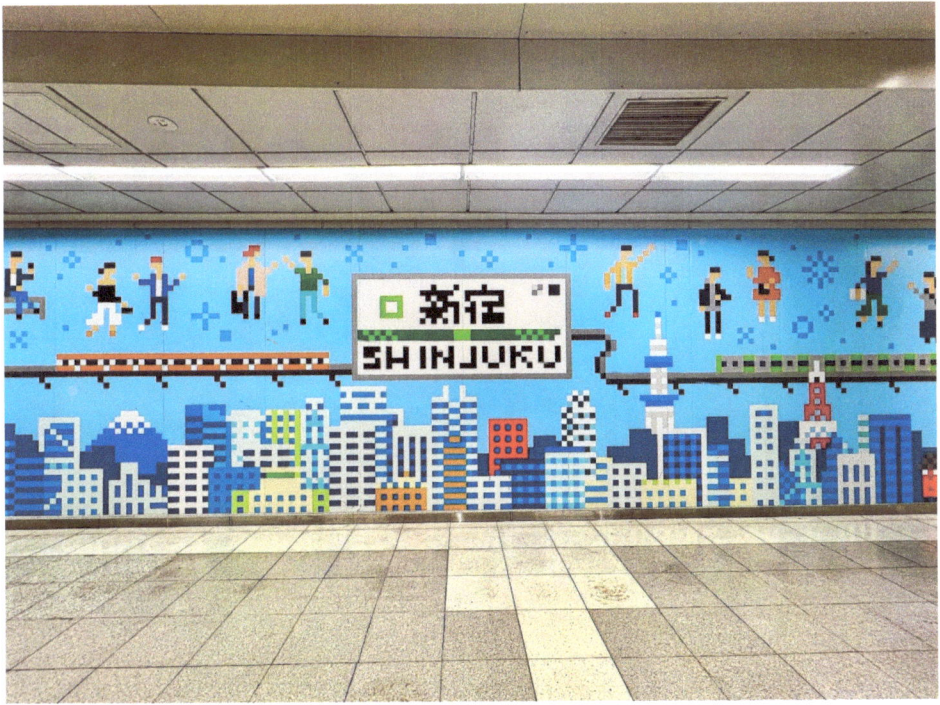

Shinjuku, Tokyo

Description:

During the day, Shinjuku is teeming with commuters, with Shinjuku Station, the world's busiest train station, acting as its major center.

SHINJUKU

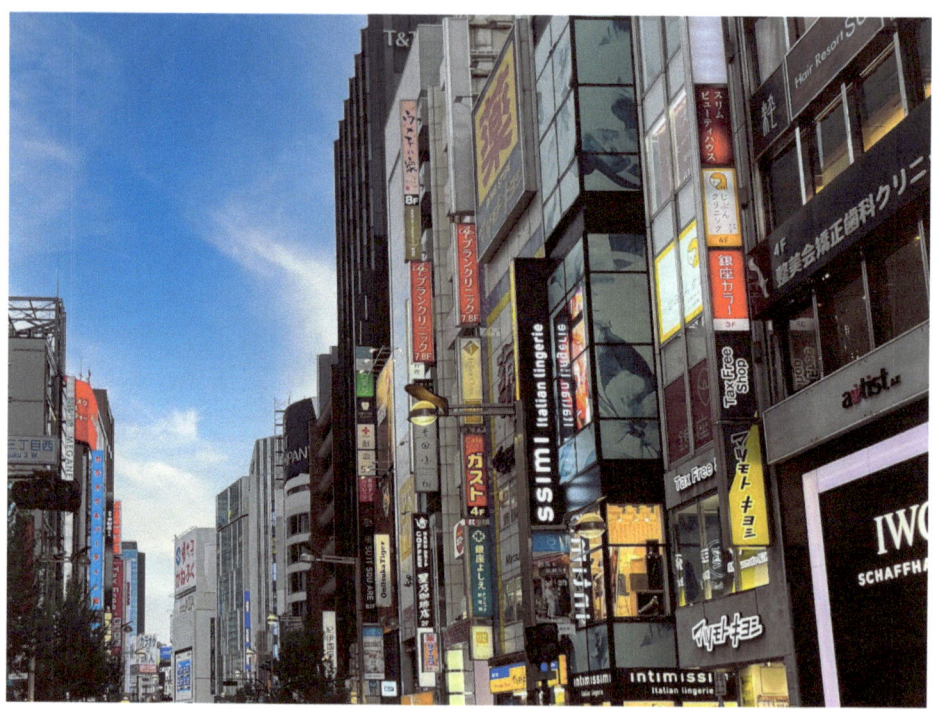

Shinjuku, Tokyo

Description:

Shoppers go to Isetan, Takashimaya, and Lumine Est, among other department shops and boutiques.

SHINJUKU CITY

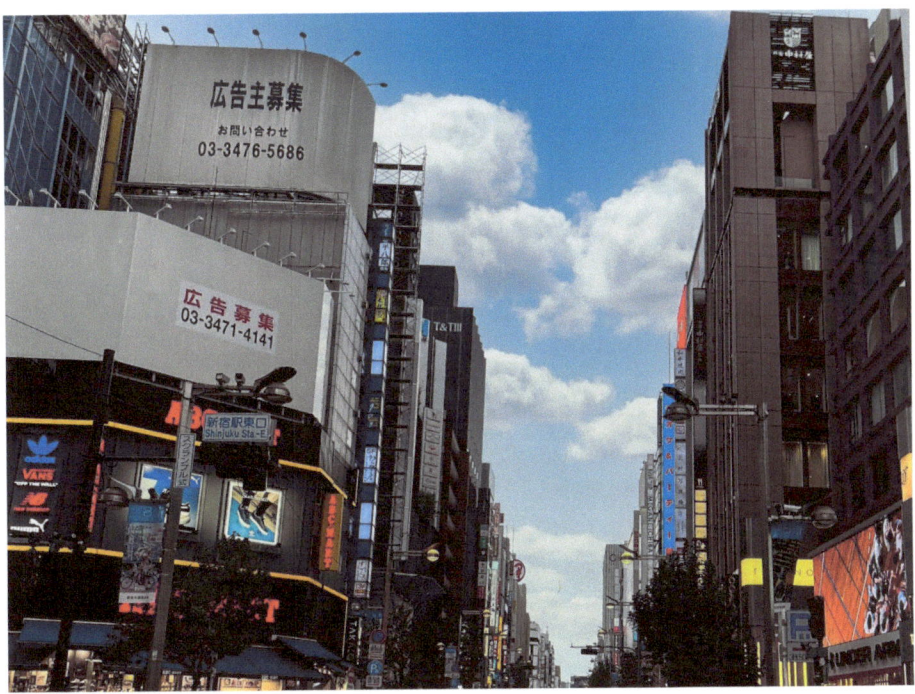

Shinjuku, Tokyo

Description:

Office workers fill the streets during lunch breaks, and you can find countless restaurants offering various cuisines to cater to their diverse tastes.

SHINJUKU NIGHT

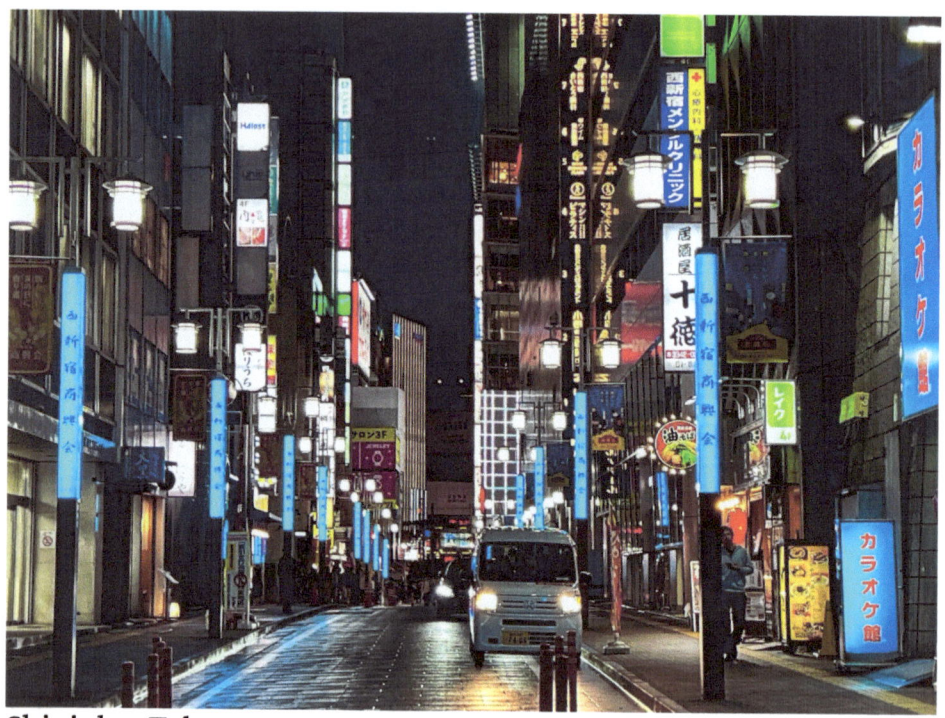

Shinjuku, Tokyo

Description:

The skyline is dominated by neon signs and high skyscrapers, giving it a visual spectacle both during the day and at night.

SHINJUKU NIGHT

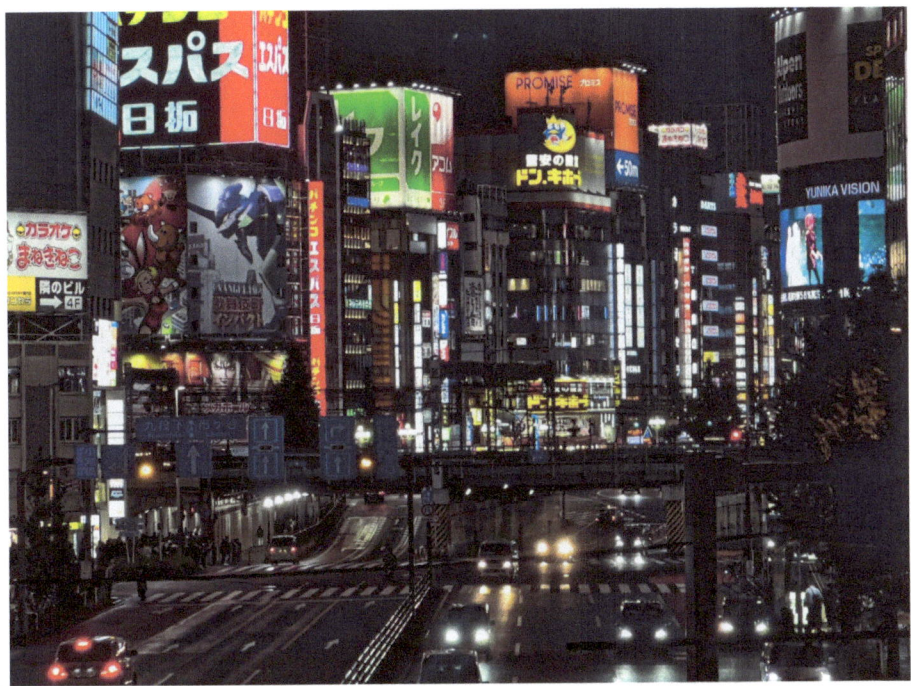

Shinjuku, Tokyo

Description:

During lunch breaks, office workers crowd the streets, and there are innumerable eateries serving a variety of cuisines to cater to their varying preferences.

SHINJUKU NIGHT

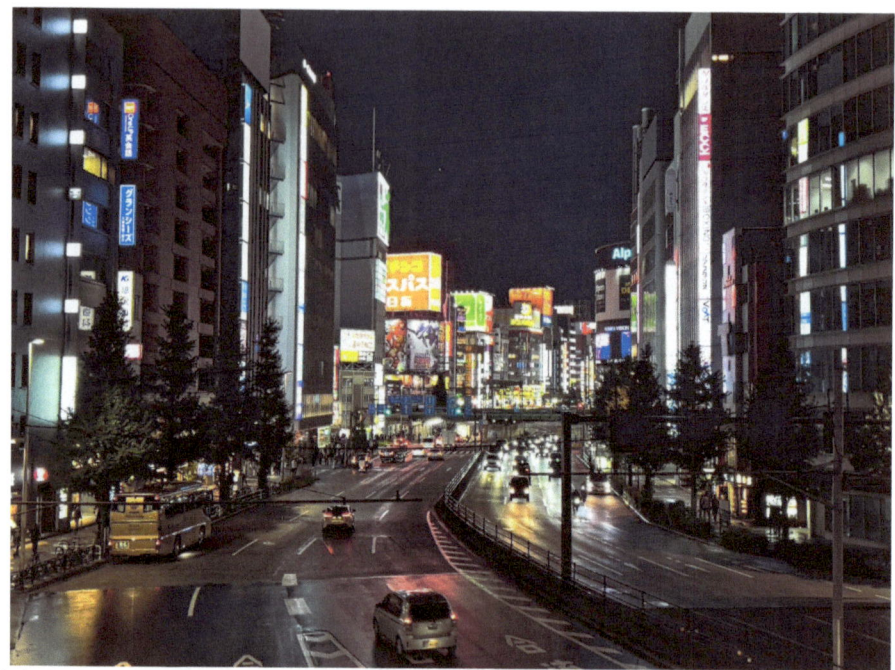

Shinjuku, Tokyo

Description:

The commercial sector is alive with corporate activity in sophisticated high-rise structures that exemplify Japan's economic power.

SHINJUKU SIDEWALK

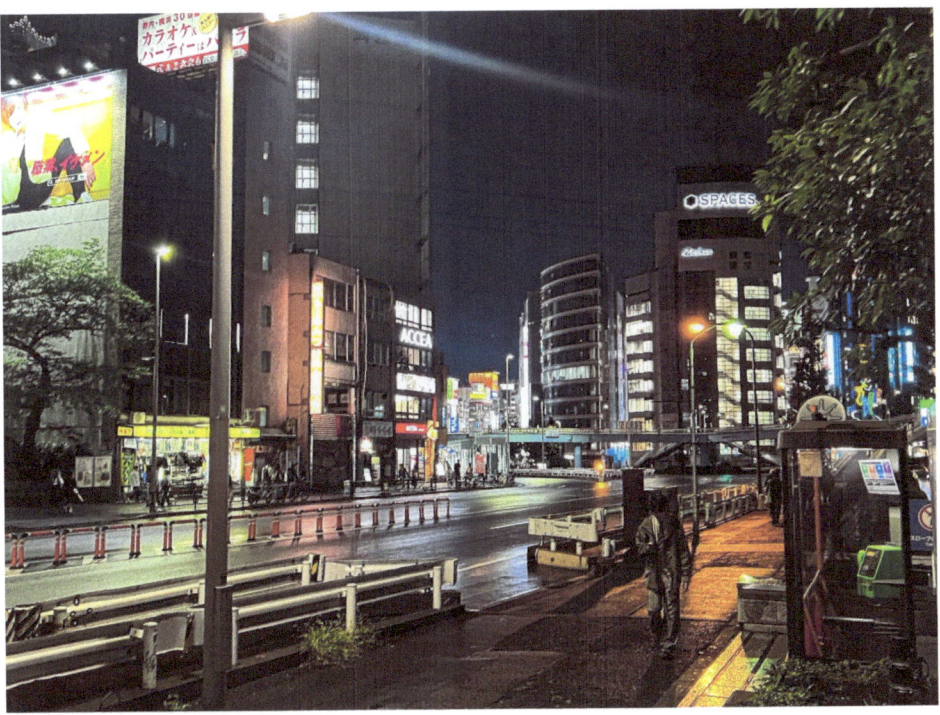

Shinjuku, Tokyo

Description:

Shinjuku is a city that never sleeps due to the dichotomy of its hectic daytime and thrilling nights.

SHINJUKU METROPOLITAN GOVERNMENT BUILDING 45F

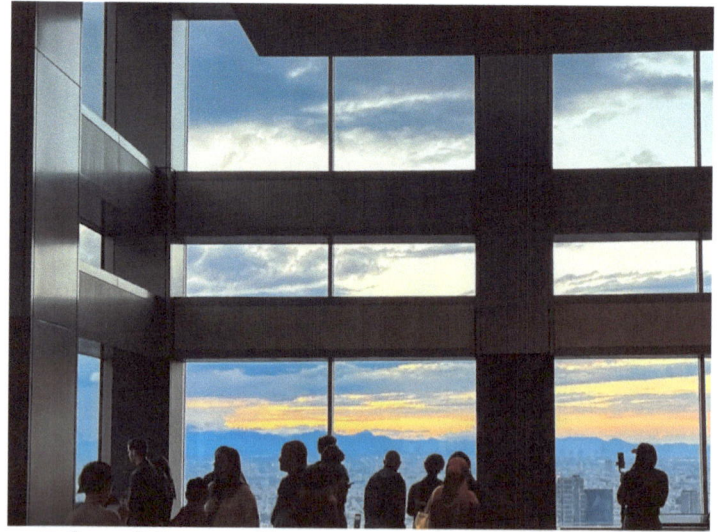

Shinjuku, Tokyo (Metropolitan Government Building)

Description:

Visitors are lured to the building's free observatories, which are placed on the 45th floors of both towers and provide stunning views of Tokyo.

SHINJUKU CITYSCAPE

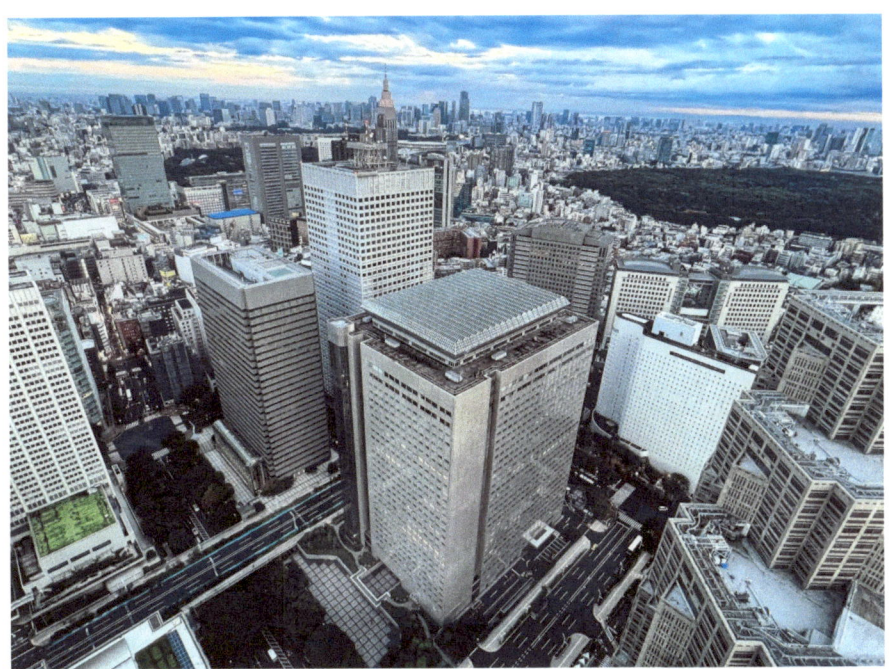

Shinjuku, Tokyo (Metropolitan Government Building)
Description:
Tourists and residents often go to the observatories, which provide an unrivaled view of the city's wide environment.

SHINJUKU CITY VIEW

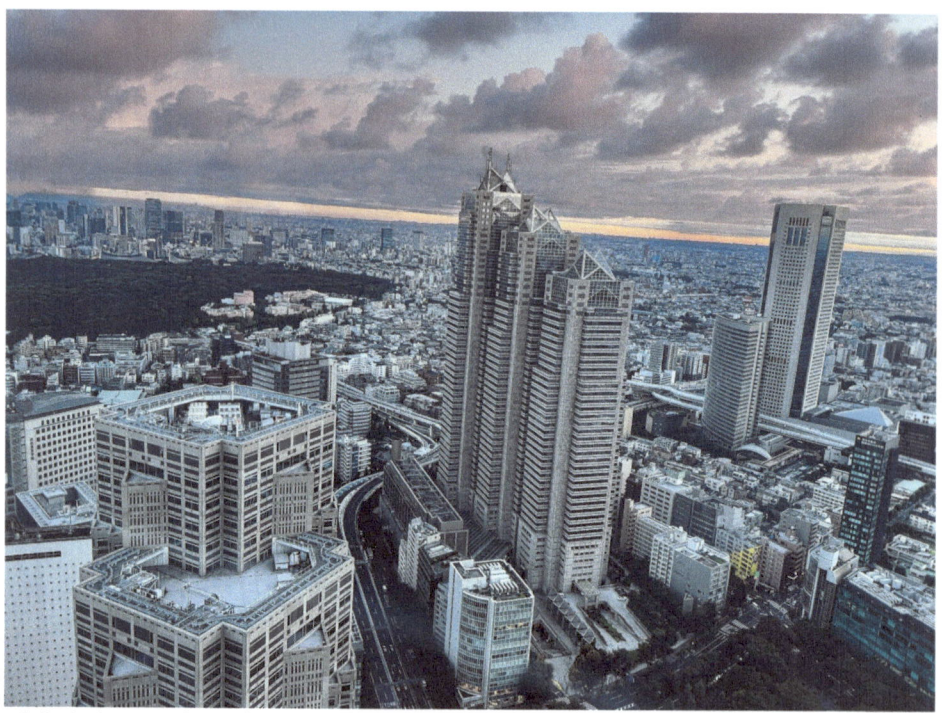

Shinjuku, Tokyo (Metropolitan Government Building)
Description:
On a clear day, one can view Mount Fuji, the Tokyo Skytree, and the breathtaking Shinjuku skyline.

SHINJUKU SUNSET

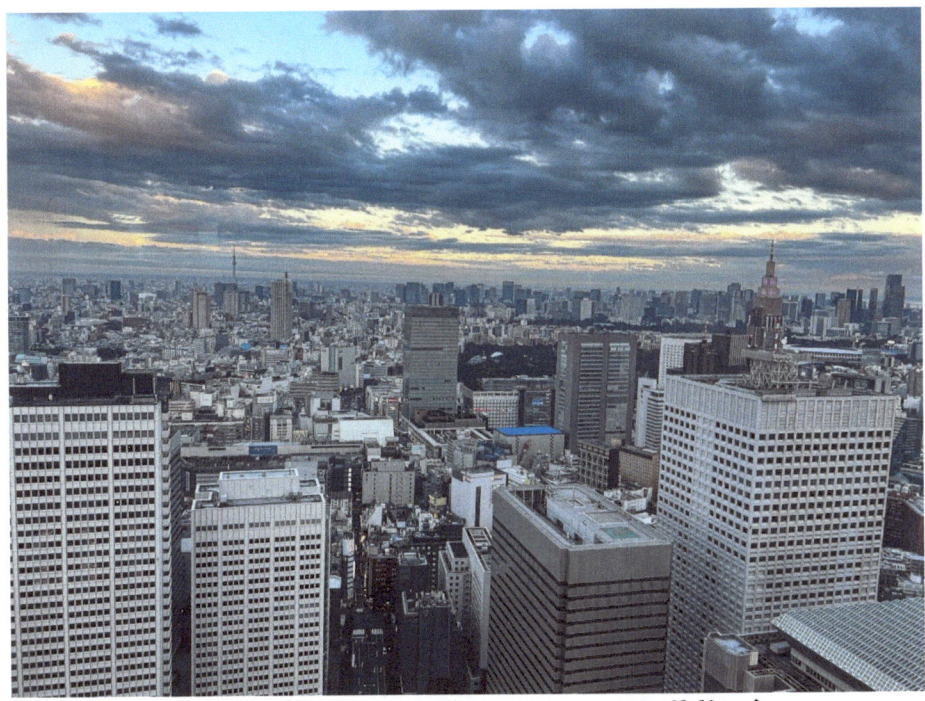

Shinjuku, Tokyo (Metropolitan Government Building)
Description:
From the observatories, you can appreciate the harmony of Shinjuku's urban environment, which blends old and new Tokyo architecture.

SHINJUKU METROPOLITAN GOVERNMENT BUILDING

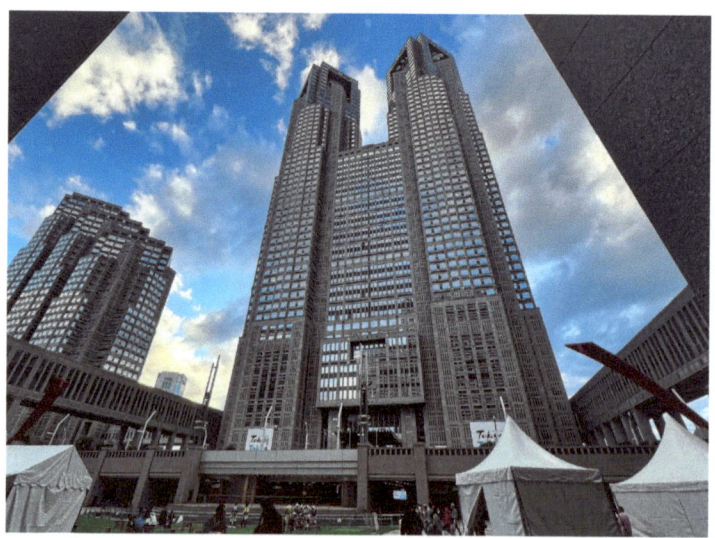

Shinjuku, Tokyo

Description:

The 243-meter-tall structure serves as the administrative head-quarters for the Tokyo Metropolitan Government.

SHINJUKU FESTIVAL FLOAT

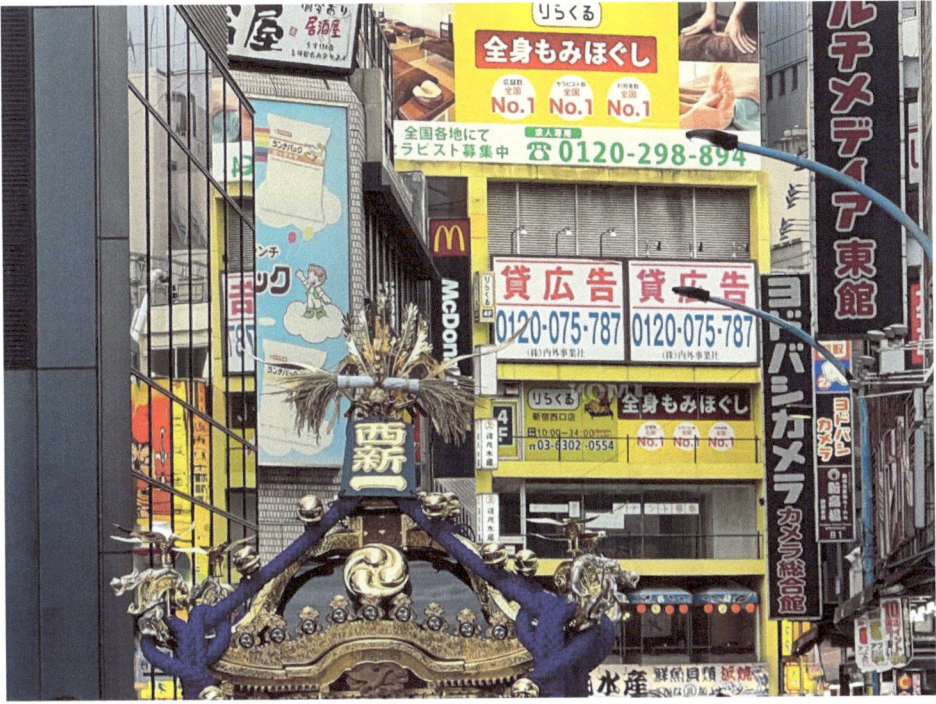

Shinjuku, Tokyo

Description:
People enjoying karaoke, pubs, clubs, and numerous themed enterprises fill the streets with energy.

AKIHABARA

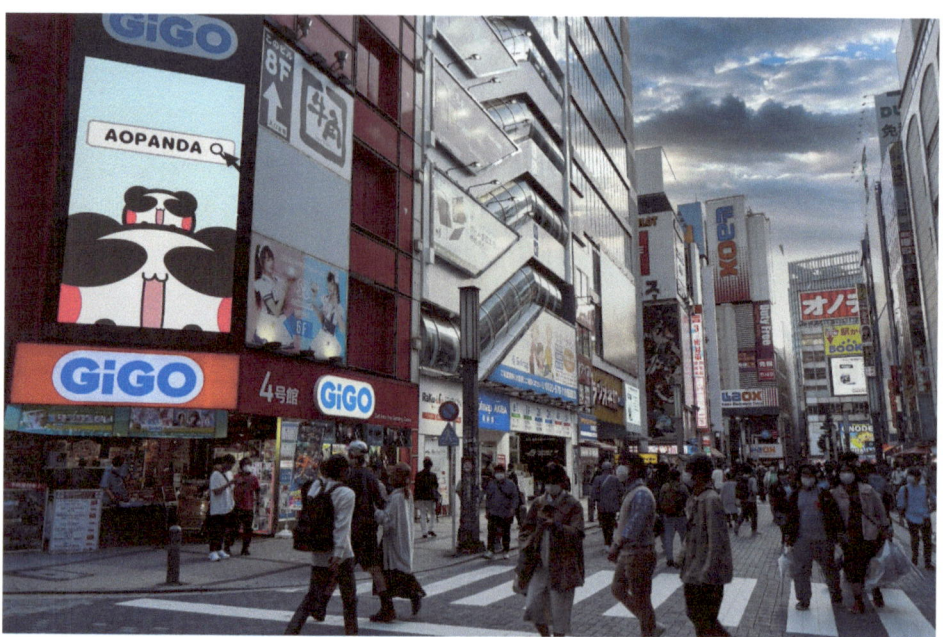

Akihabara, Tokyo

Description:

This is the Akihabara district, which is a haven for anime and electronics fans.

AKIHABARA STATION

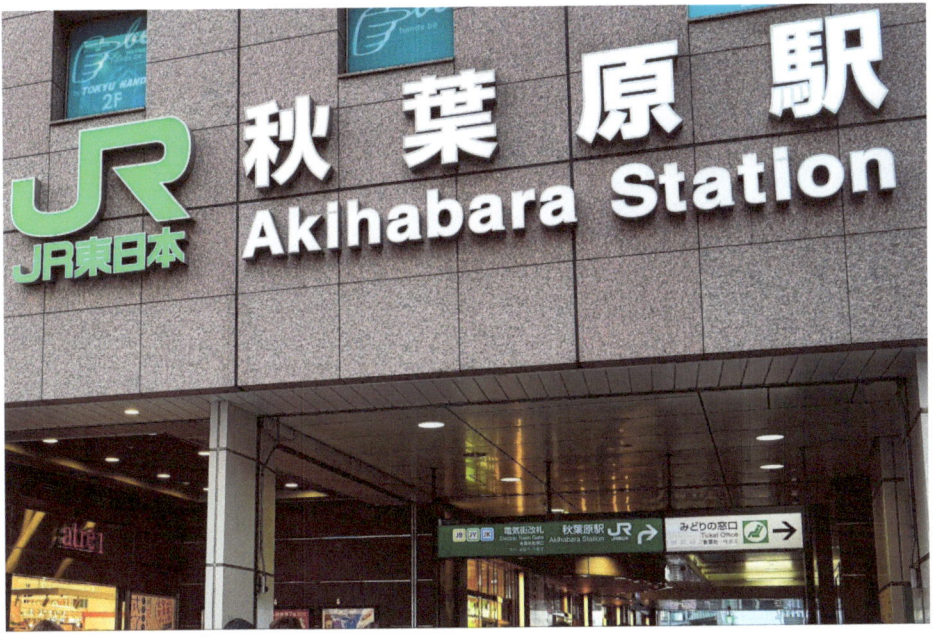

Akihabara, Tokyo

Description:

Akihabara Station is a major transportation hub in Tokyo's heart. The platforms at the station have helpful signage and directions. The staff at the station is friendly and used to assisting tourists.

AKIHABARA STREET PERFORMER

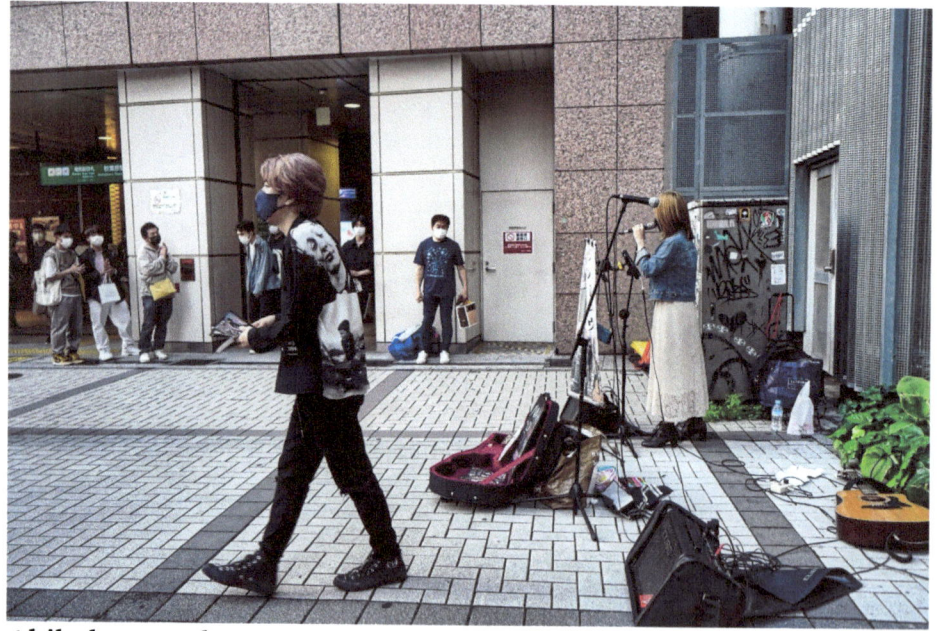

Akihabara, Tokyo

Description:

The station is well-known for its bustling atmosphere, which is populated by commuters, tourists, and shoppers. The district is known for its quirky and unique street performances.

AKIHABARA STATION WALL ART

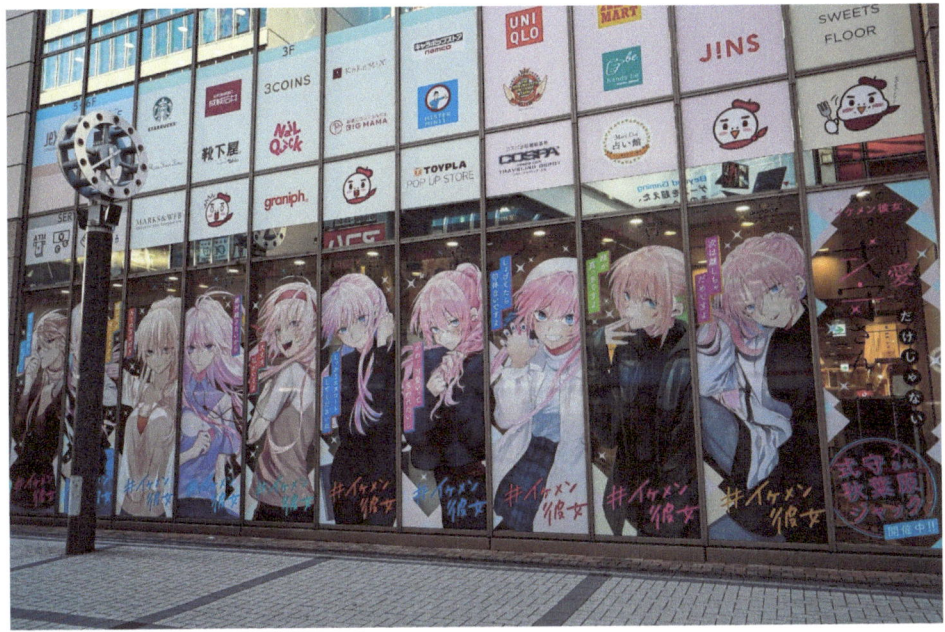

Akihabara, Tokyo

Description:

Colorful signs and advertisements greet visitors to Akihabara Station.

AKIHABARA CROSSING

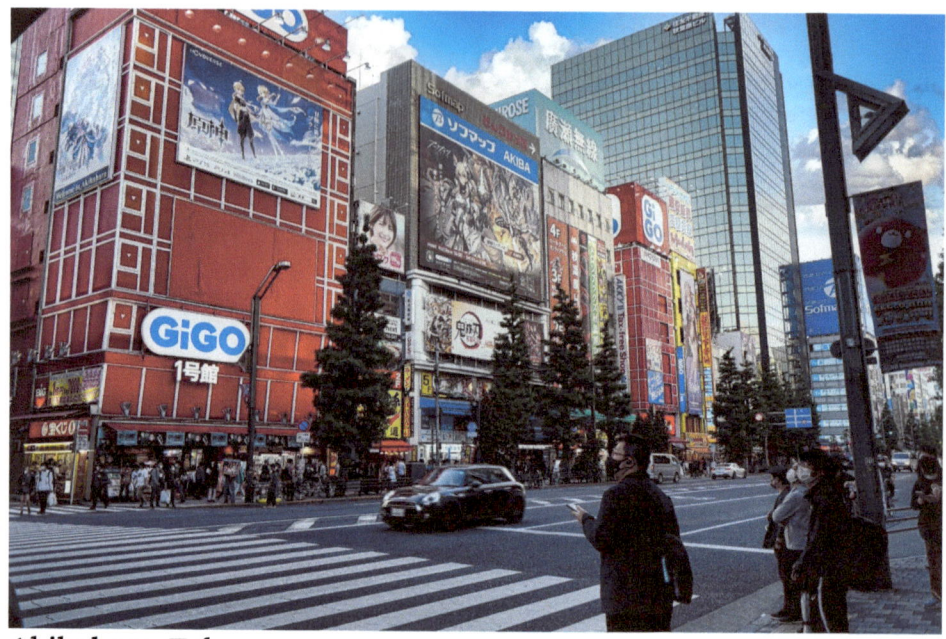

Akihabara, Tokyo

Description:

Because of the abundance of electronic stores, Akihabara is often referred to as "Electric Town."

AKIHABARA BRIDGE

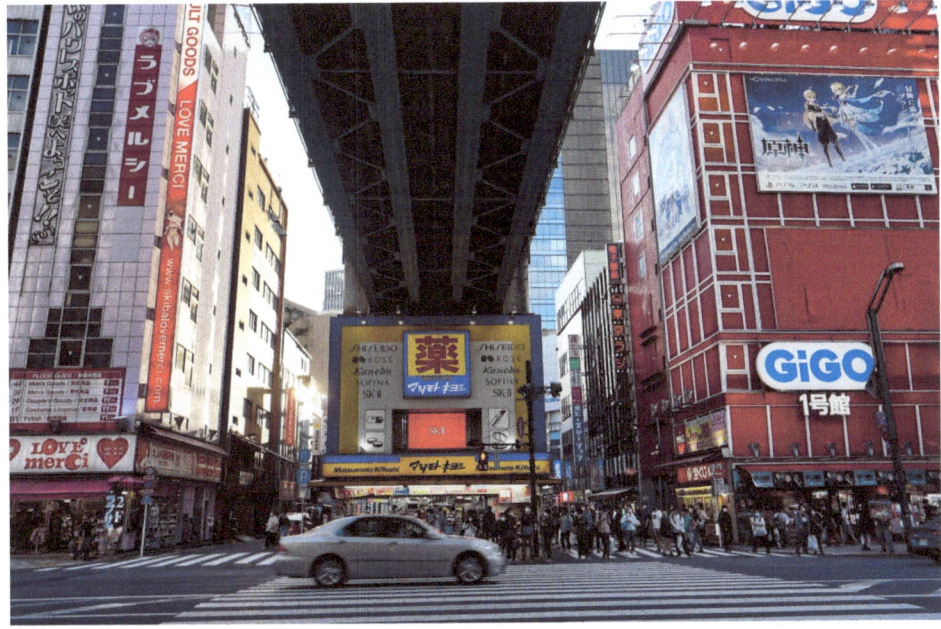

Akihabara, Tokyo

Description:

Akihabara connects commuters to Tokyo's vast rail network while immersing them in the lively atmosphere of the surrounding district.

AKIHABARA BUILDING

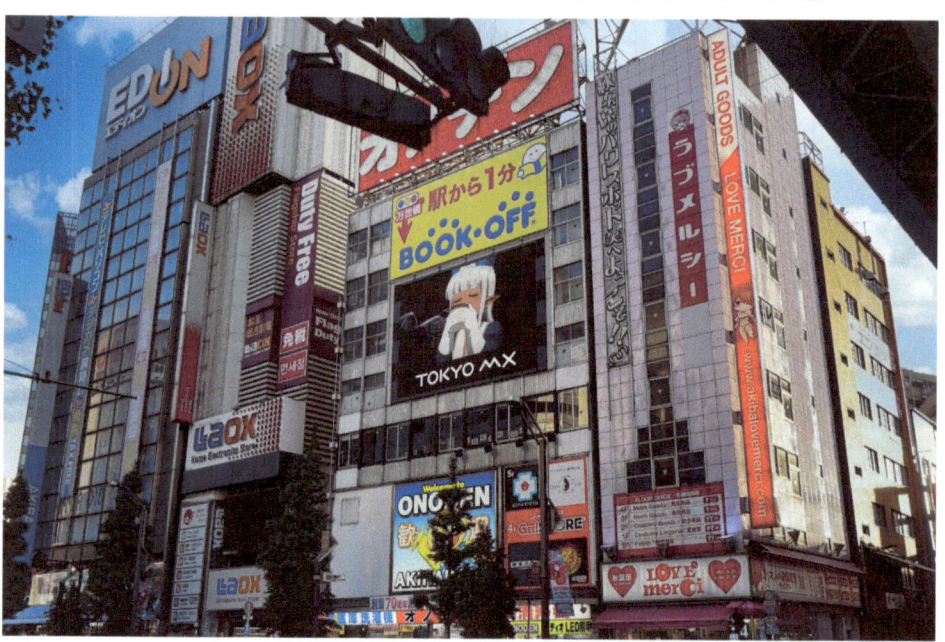

Akihabara, Tokyo

Description:

The district is a center for otaku culture, with shops and restaurants.

AKIHABARA

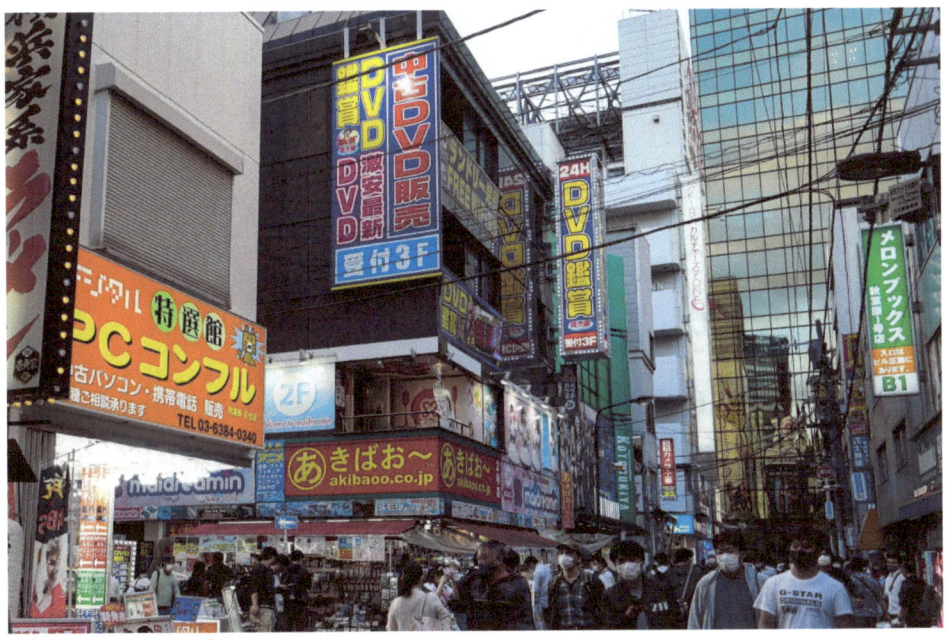

Akihabara, Tokyo

Description:

The area surrounding Akihabara is always bustling with activity.

AKIHABARA ALLEY

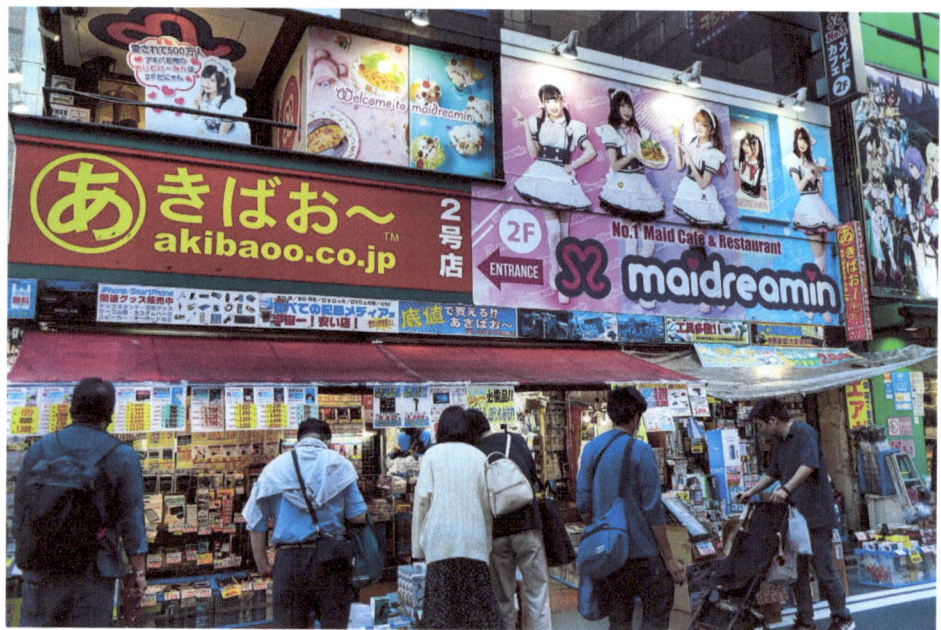

Akihabara, Tokyo

Description:

Akihabara is well-known for its maid cafes, where waitresses dress up as maids and serve customers.

AKIHABARA SHOP

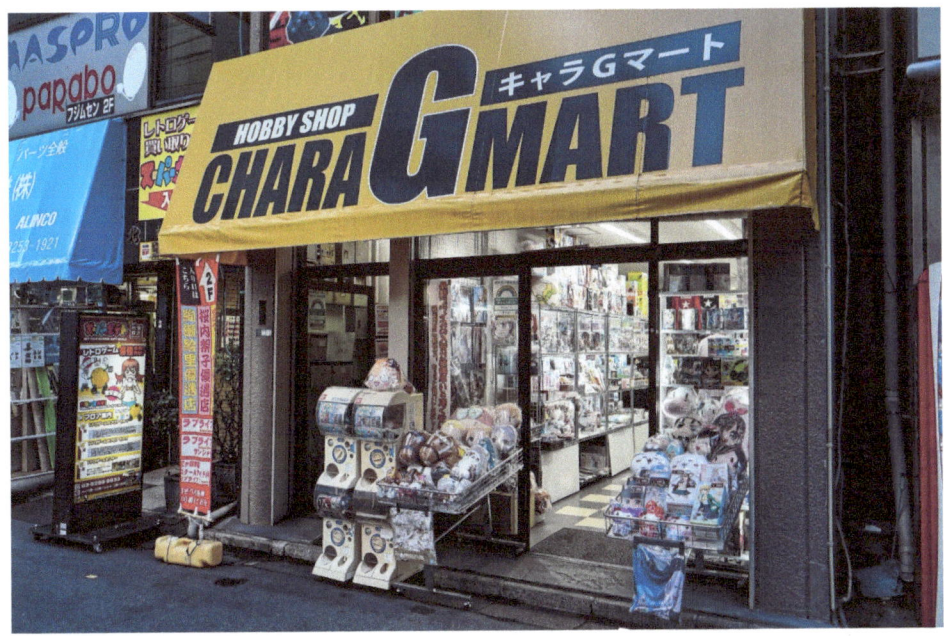

Akihabara, Tokyo

Description:

Akihabara is a paradise for collectors, with shops selling rare and vintage electronics.

AKIHABARA
BUSY ALLEY

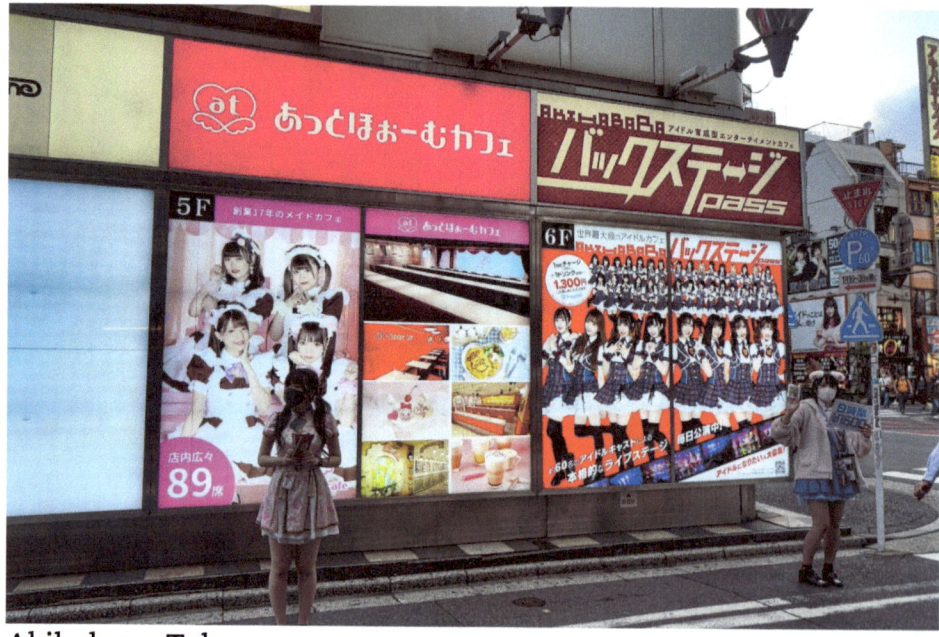

Akihabara, Tokyo

Description:

Visitors often find themselves immersed in the vibrant subculture of Akihabara.

AKIHABARA CAFE

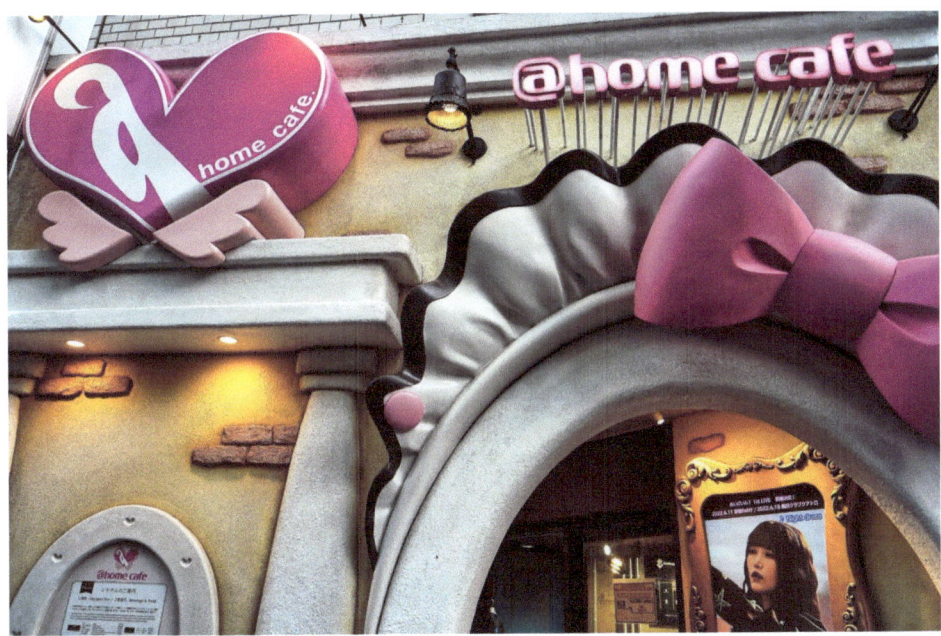

Akihabara, Tokyo

Description:

Akihabara is a must-visit destination for those interested in Japanese pop culture.

AKIHABARA BIC CAMERA

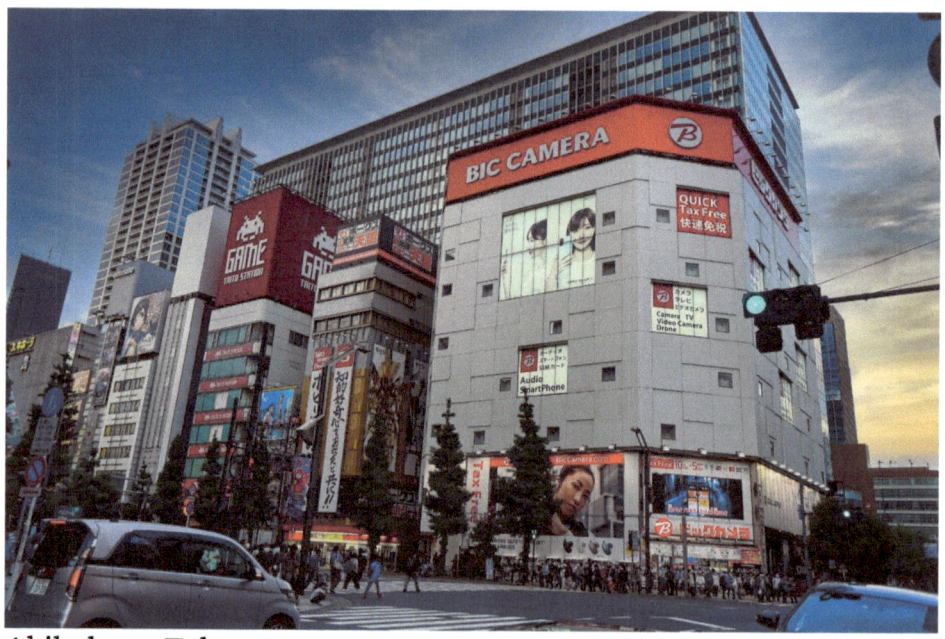

Akihabara, Tokyo

Description:

Akihabara Station is a fantastic place to purchase electronics and gadgets.

AKIHABARA BIC CAMERA

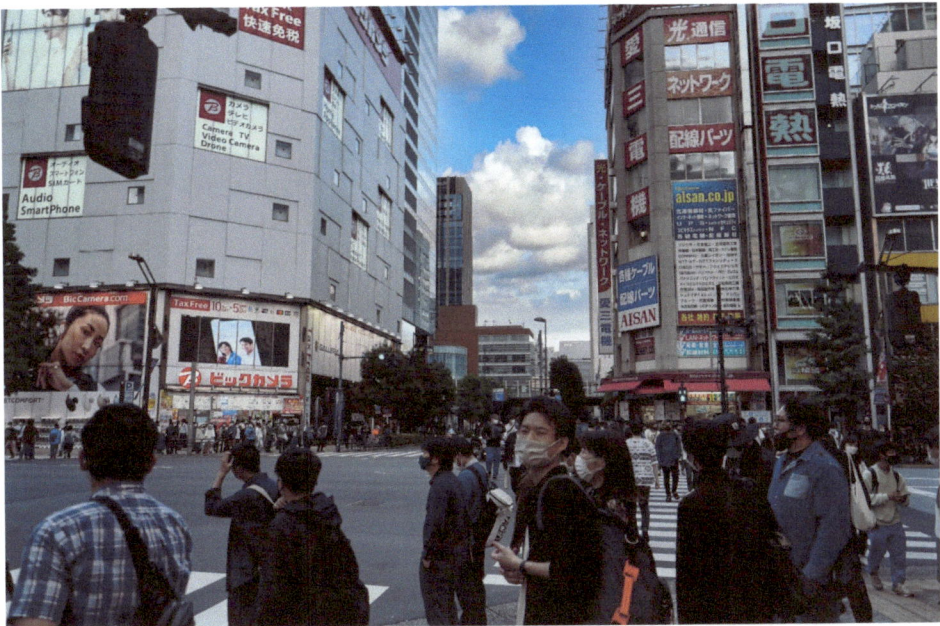

Akihabara, Tokyo

Description:

The platforms at Akihabara Station are always crowded with commuters and shoppers.

AKIHABARA STREET

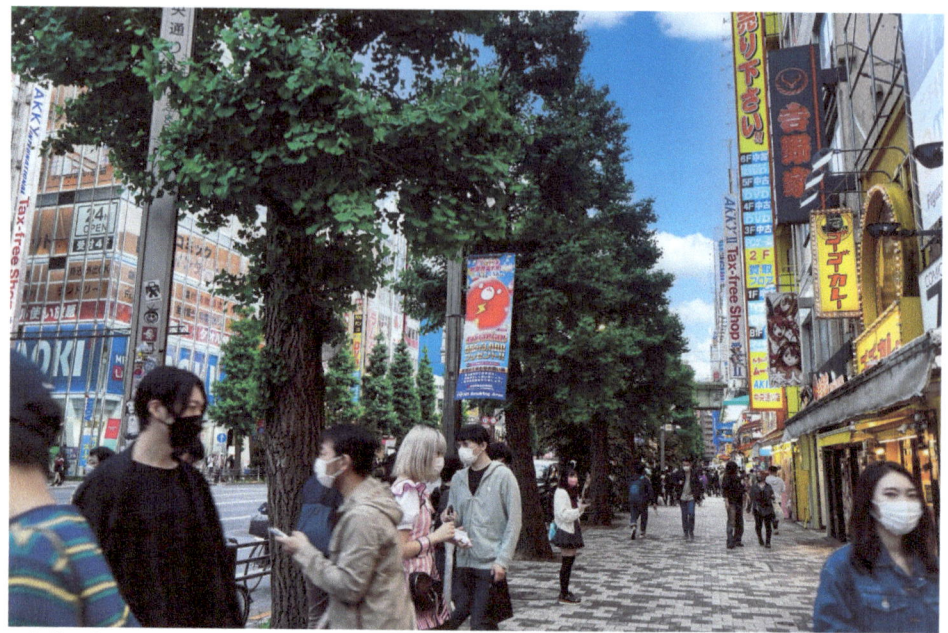

Akihabara, Tokyo

Description:

Akihabara embodies Tokyo's dynamic spirit, with its constant hustle and bustle of commuters and travelers. You can spot cosplayers in elaborate costumes wandering the streets.

AKIHABARA ROAD CROSSING

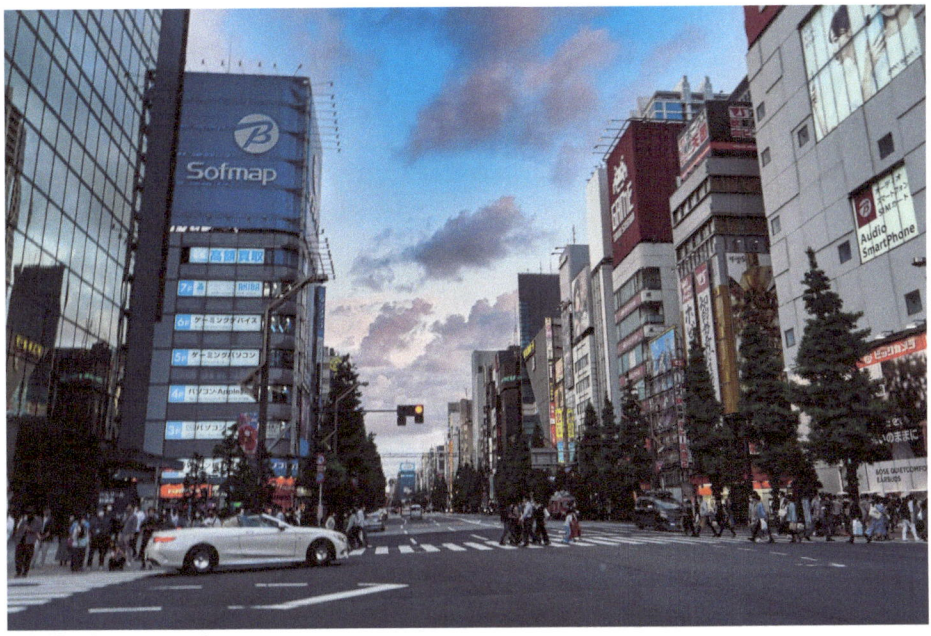

Akihabara, Tokyo

Description:

There are several multi-story hobby shops in Akihabara, each with its own specialty.

AKIHABARA BUSY STREET

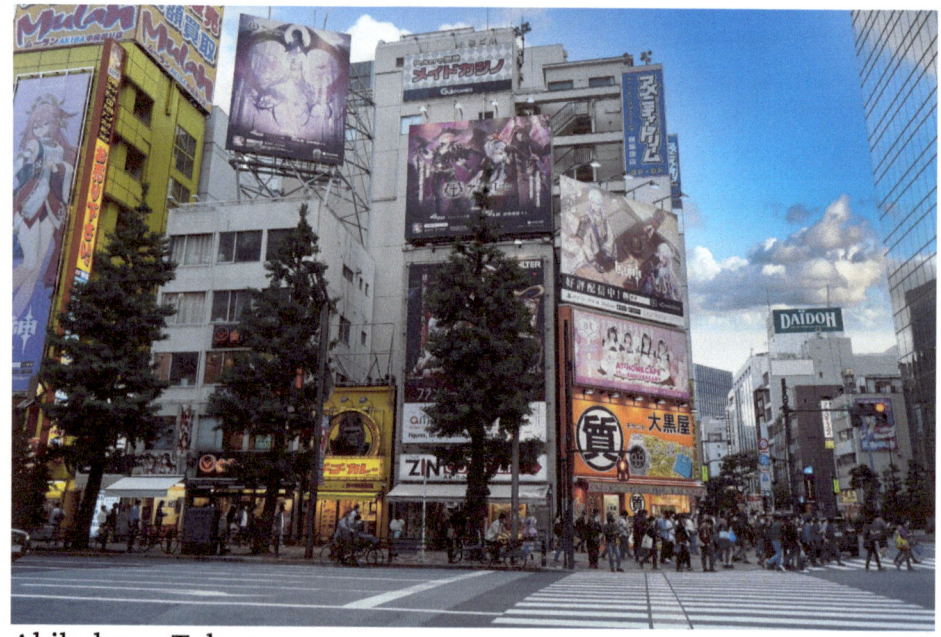

Akihabara, Tokyo

Description:

The station is surrounded by tall buildings that house shops and cafes.

AKIHABARA BIC CAMERA FRONT ENTRANCE

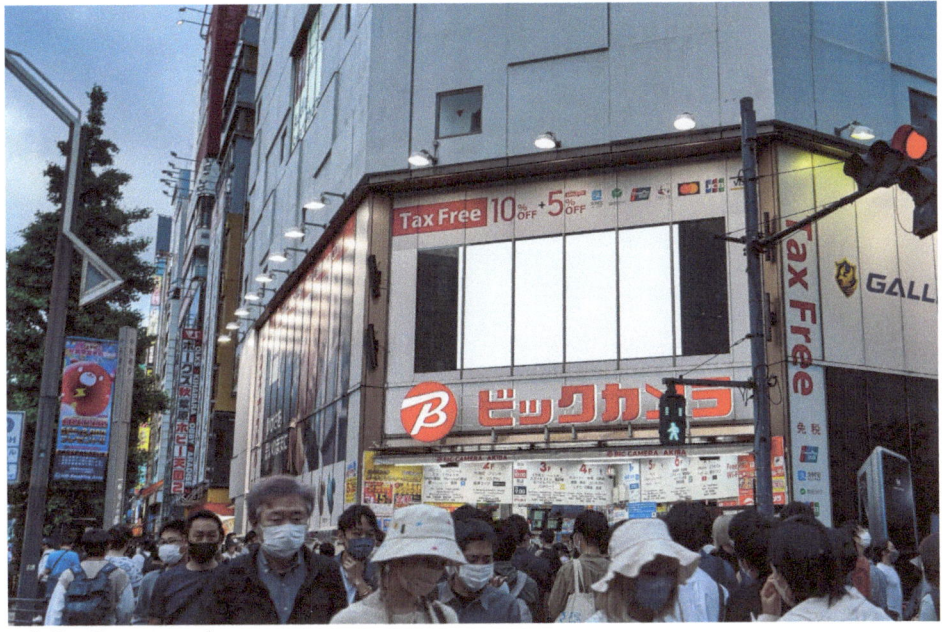

Akihabara, Tokyo

Description:

The streets of Akihabara are lined with shops selling used and collectible items.

AKIHABARA BIC CAMERA DISPLAY

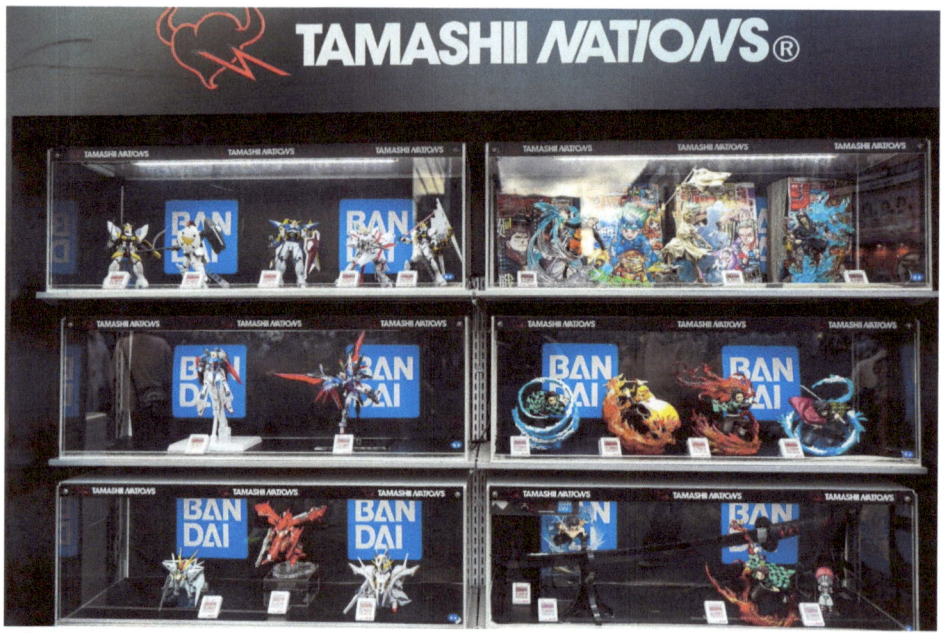

Akihabara, Tokyo

Description:

Akihabara is a collector's paradise, with shops selling rare and vintage electronics.

AKIHABARA STREETS CROSSING

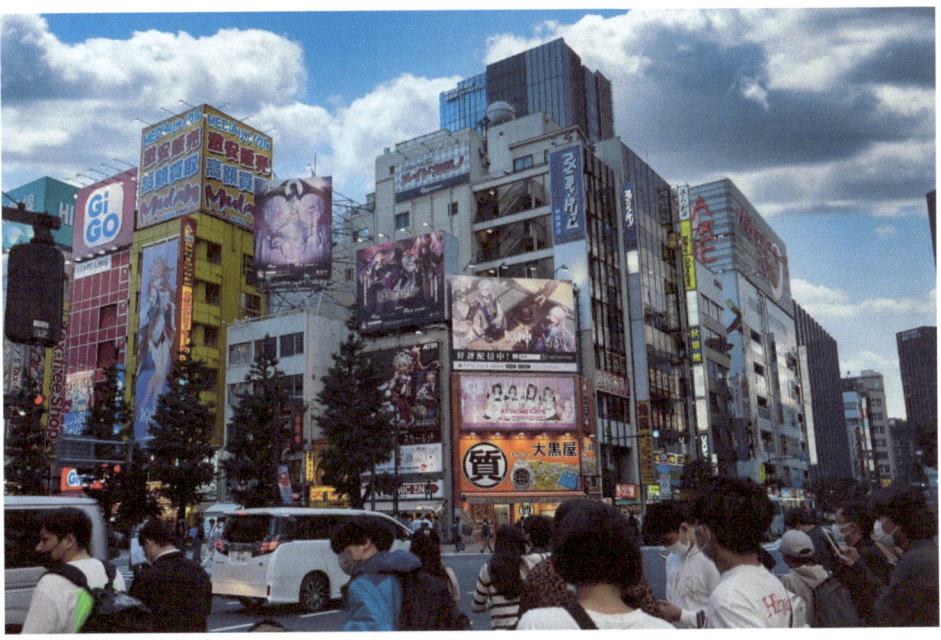

Akihabara, Tokyo

Description:

There are shops selling merchandise from Japanese pop idols.

AKIHABARA
BIC CAMERA
CAPSULE TOYS

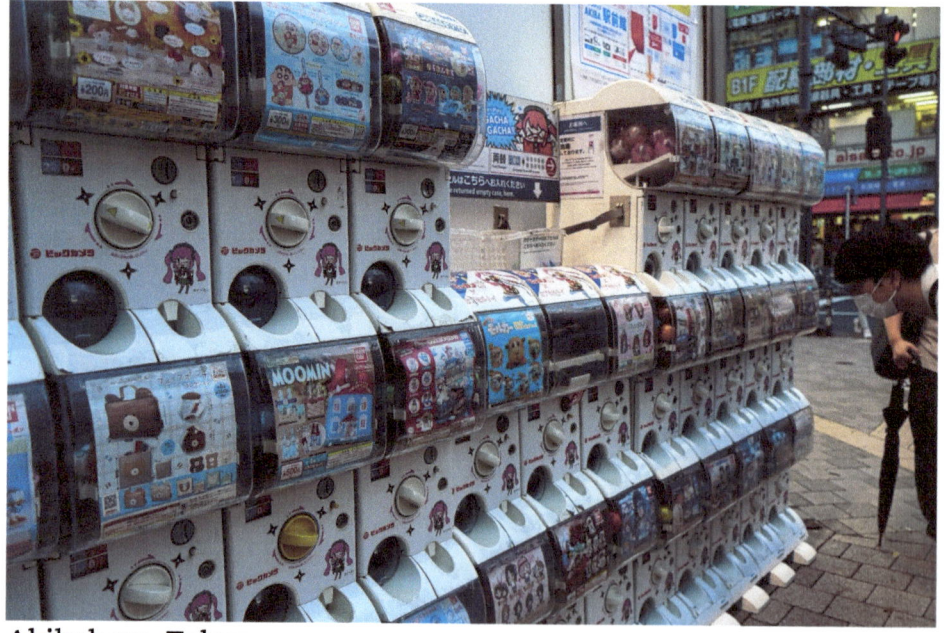

Akihabara, Tokyo

Description:

It is simple to locate shops devoted to specific anime series or video game franchises.

AKIHABARA STREETS WALKING

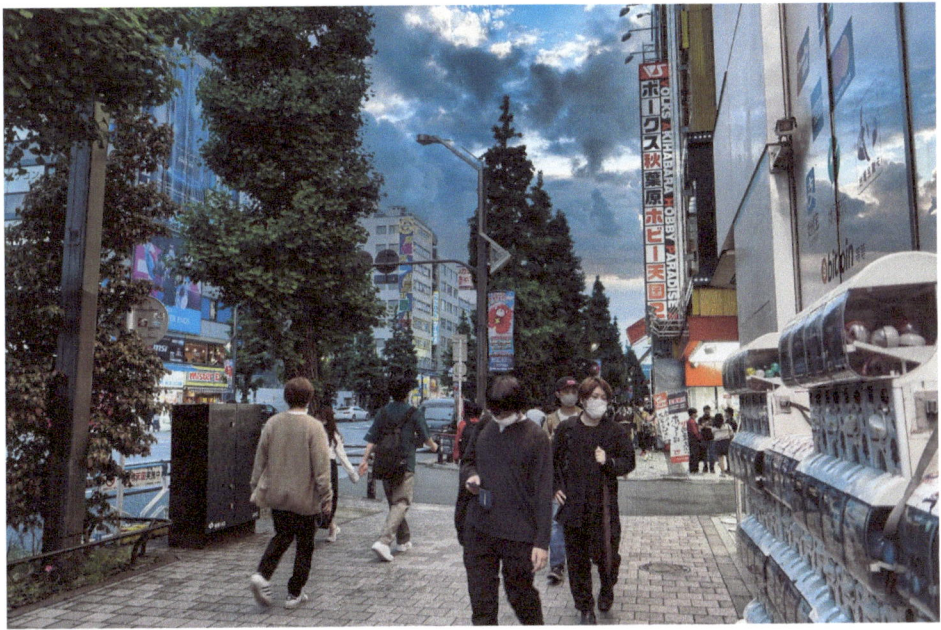

Akihabara, Tokyo

Description:

There are shops in the area that sell retro gaming consoles, capsule toys, and games.

AKIHABARA STANDING POSTERS

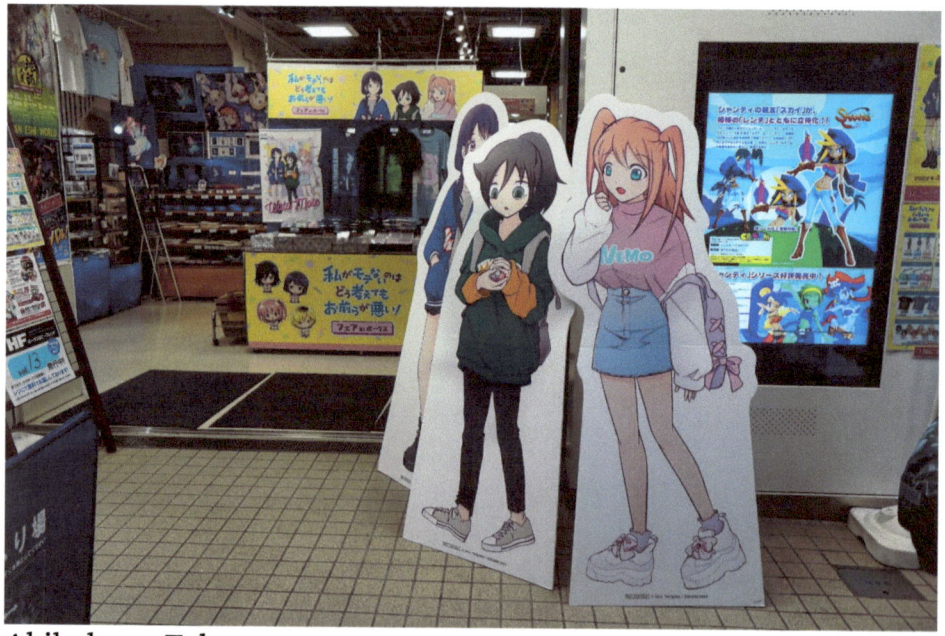

Akihabara, Tokyo

Description:

Anime fans will find a plethora of merchandise, ranging from figurines to posters.

AKIHABARA
STANDING POSTER

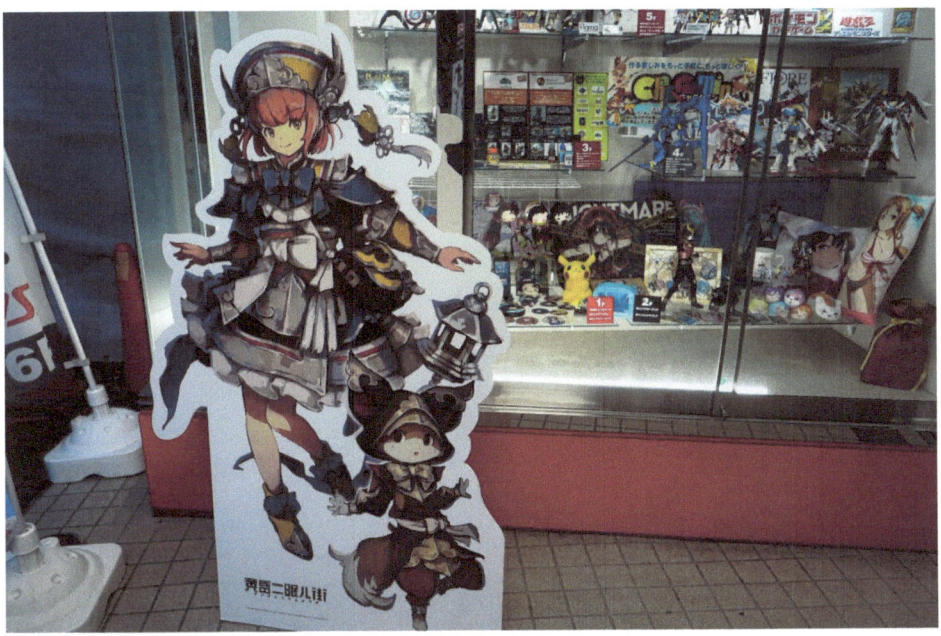

Akihabara, Tokyo

Description:

Pop-up events and limited-edition merchandise releases are popular in Akihabara.

AKIHABARA EVENING

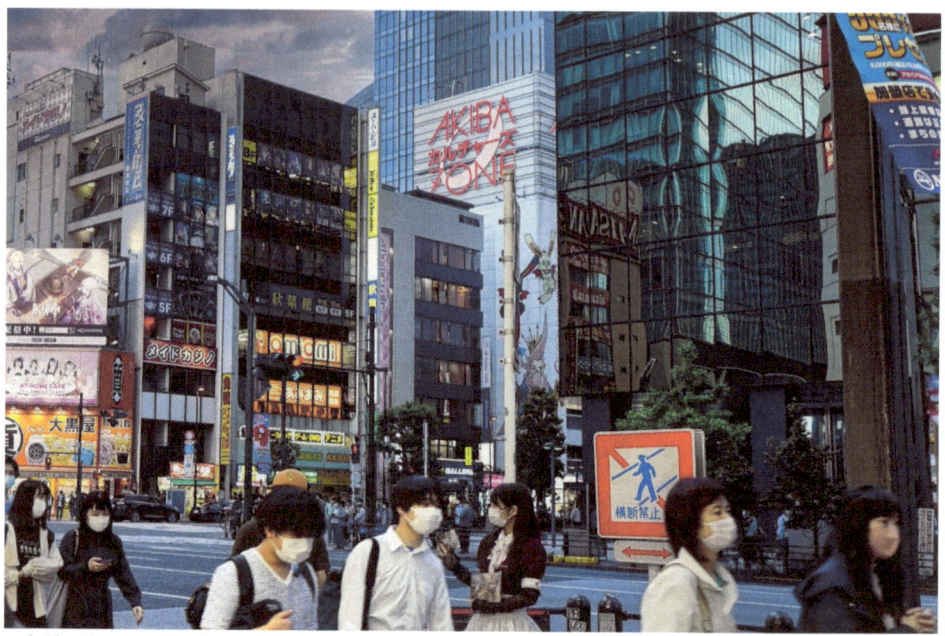

Akihabara, Tokyo

Description:

Japanese pop culture can be experienced in a variety of forms.

AKIHABARA GAME CENTER TAITO STATION

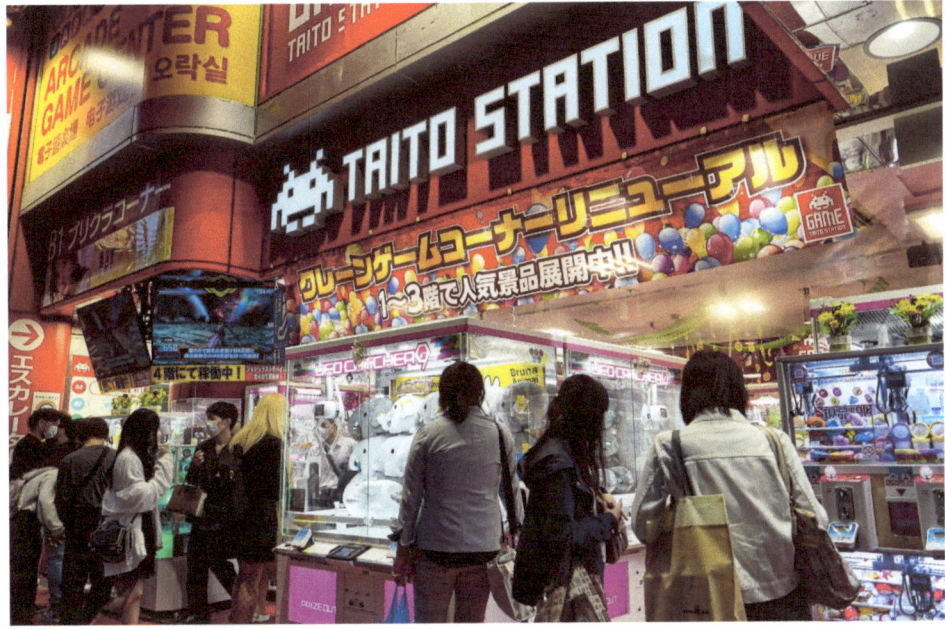

Akihabara, Tokyo

Description:

Akihabara is also well-known for its many arcades, where gamers can enjoy a wide range of games.

AKIHABARA DVD GAME SHOP

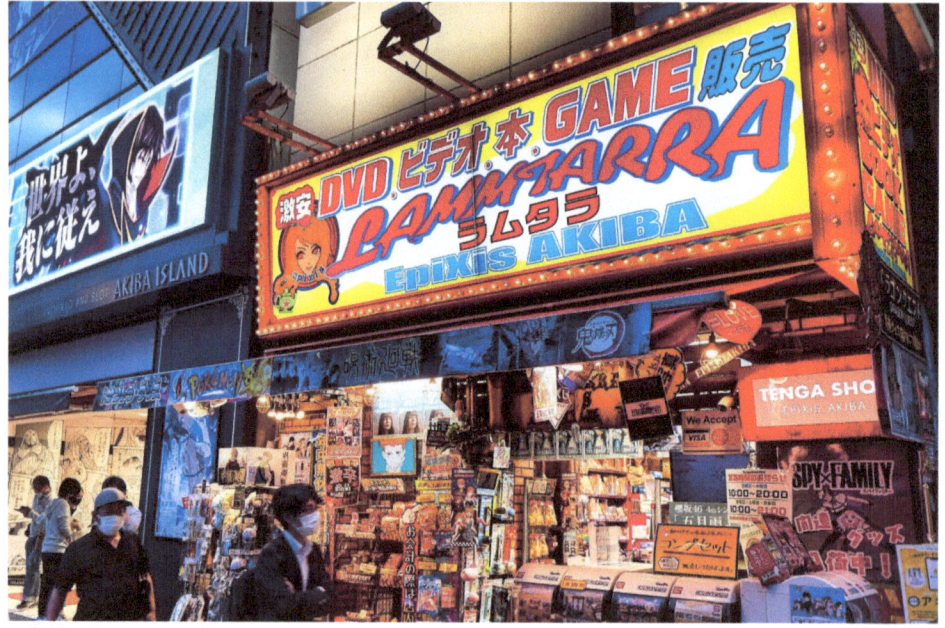

Akihabara, Tokyo

Description:
Japanese pop culture can be experienced in a variety of forms.

AKIHABARA AD

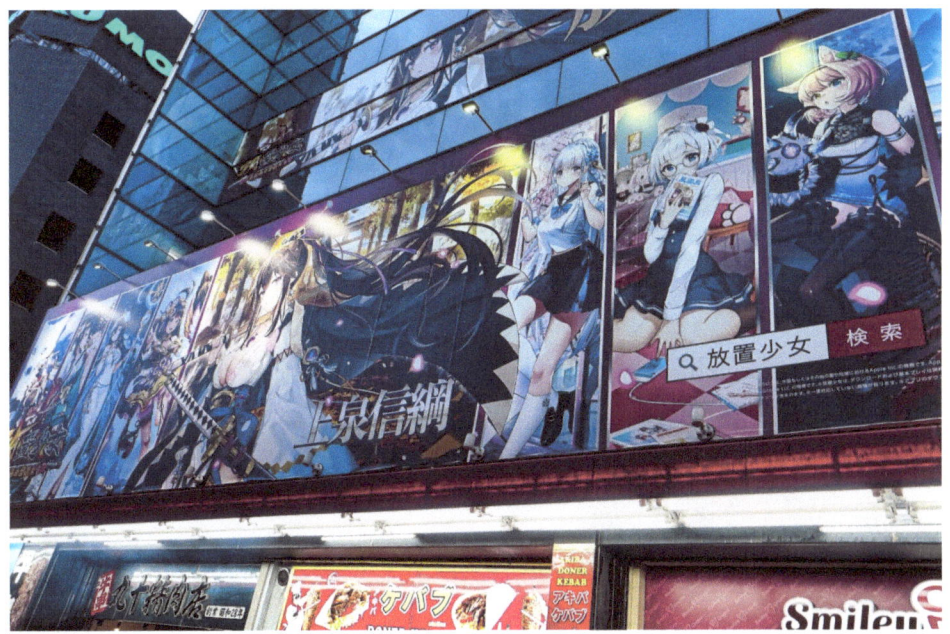

Akihabara, Tokyo

Description:
The station's exterior is adorned with larger-than-life billboards.

AKIHABARA
KEBAB SHOP

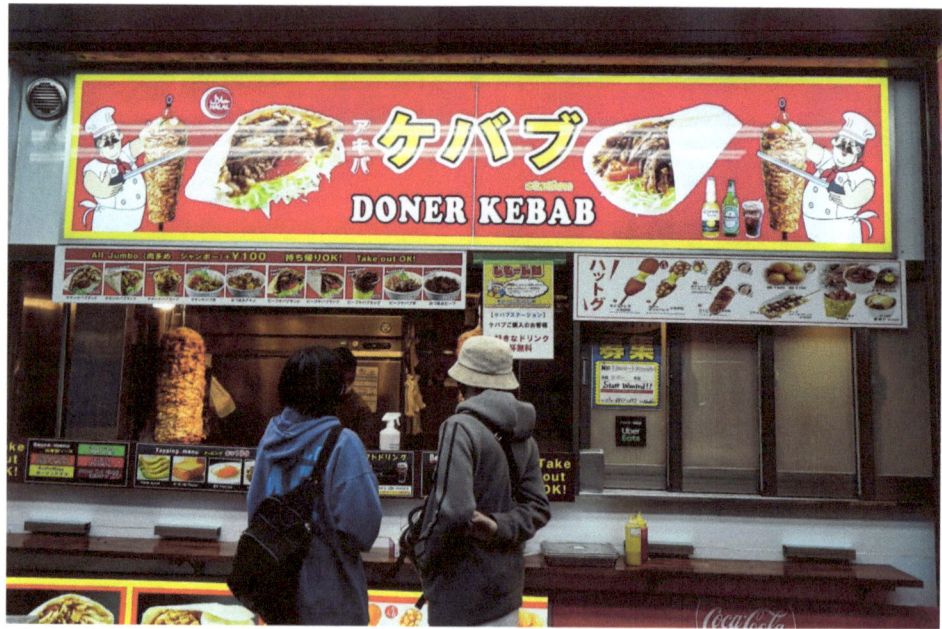

Akihabara, Tokyo

Description:

Akihabara also has a plethora of cafes and restaurants catering to a wide range of tastes.

AKIHABARA AD VIEW

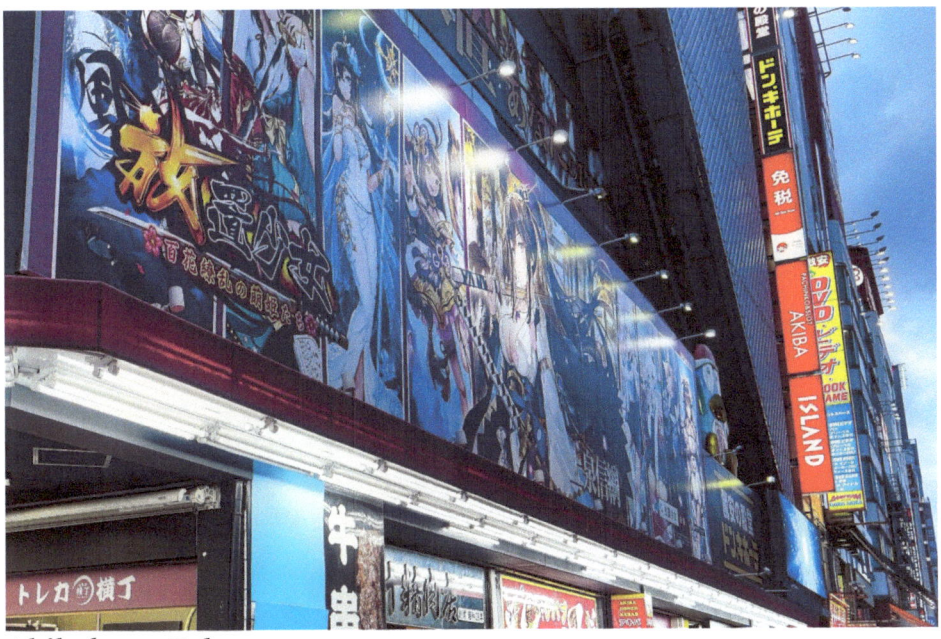

Akihabara, Tokyo

Description:

 Because of its central location, the station is an excellent starting point for exploring Tokyo.

AKIHABARA STREET WALKING

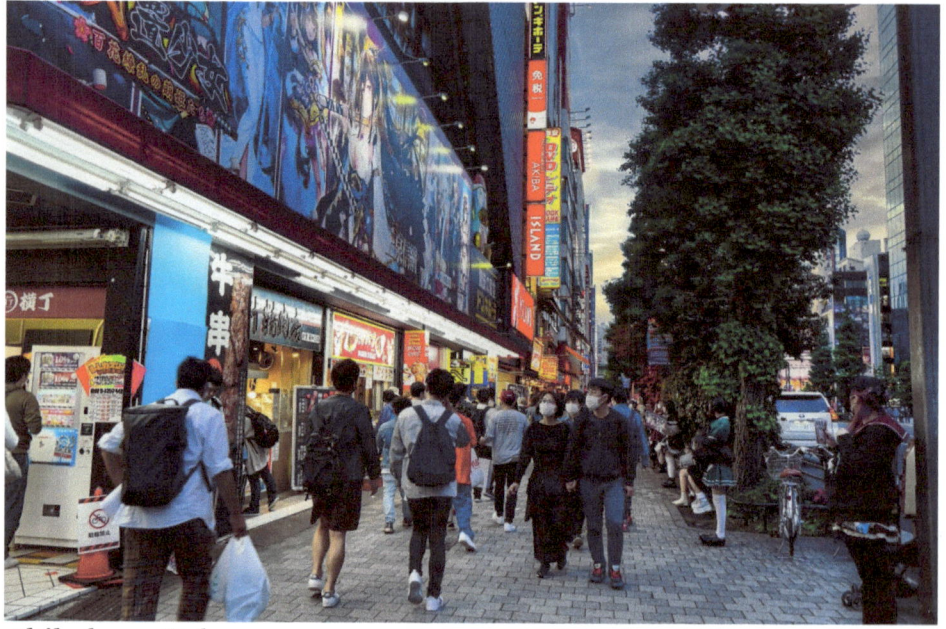

Akihabara, Tokyo

Description:
Akihabara has a distinctive retro-futuristic design with colorful neon lights.

DON QUIJOTE
AKIHABARA

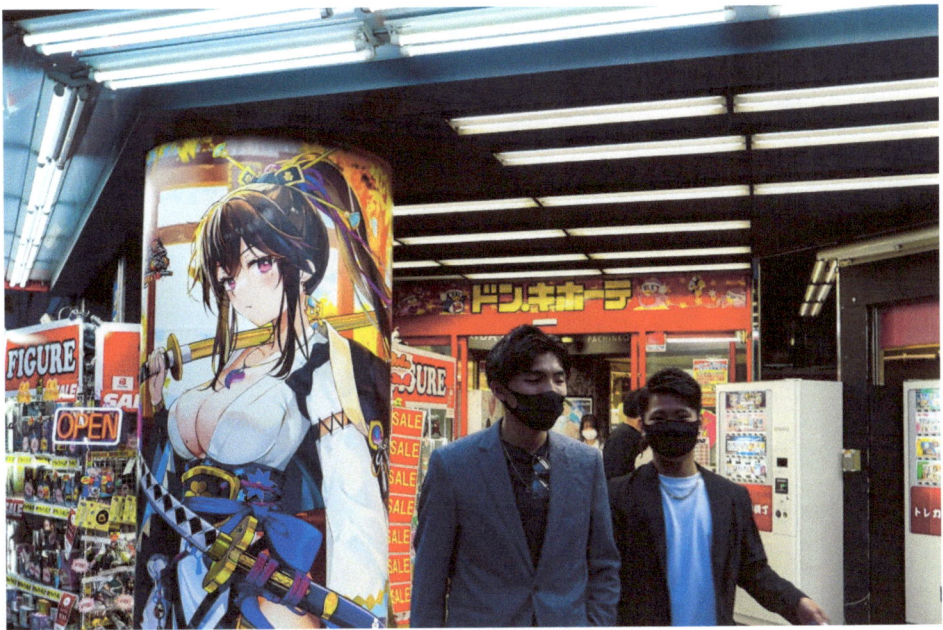

Akihabara, Tokyo

Description:

For fans of both classic and modern video games, Akihabara is a treasure trove. There are shops selling unusual collectibles and paraphernalia.

AKIHABARA DON QUIJOTE ACROSS THE STREET

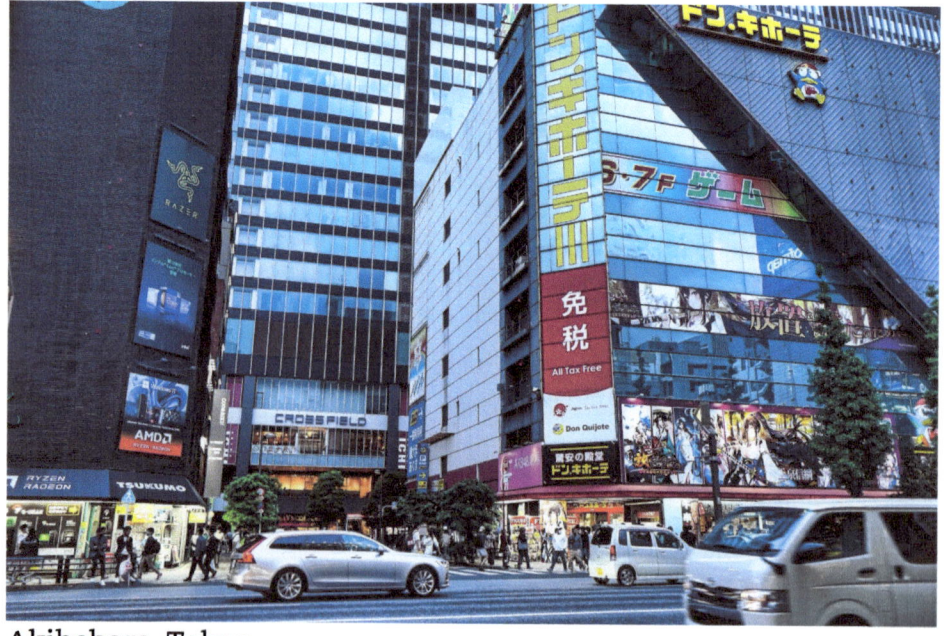

Akihabara, Tokyo

Description:

The architecture of the district combines modern and traditional elements.

AKIHABARA BIG AD

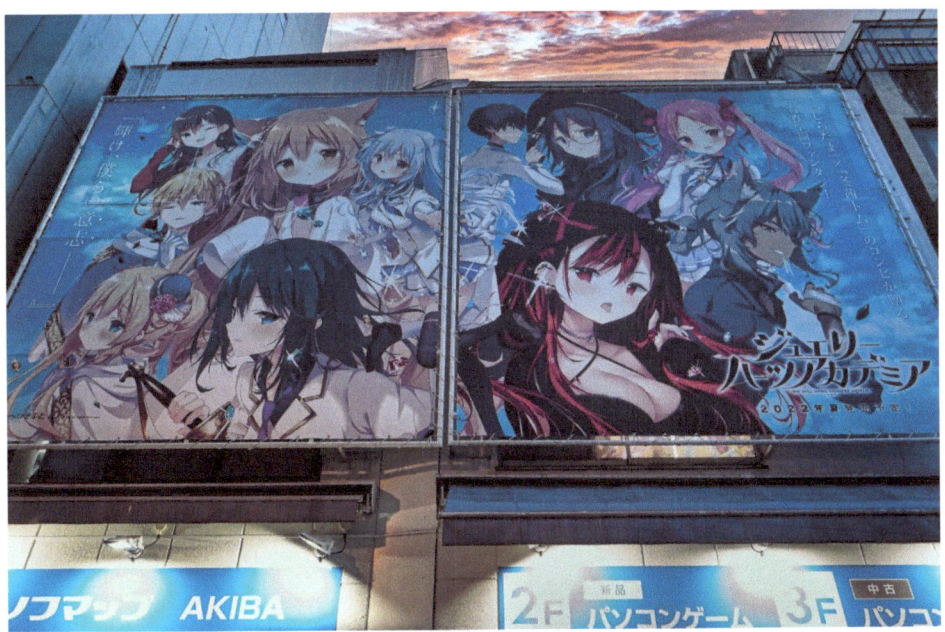

Akihabara, Tokyo

Description:

With its bright signs and bustling streets, the district comes alive at night.

AKIHABARA SHOPS

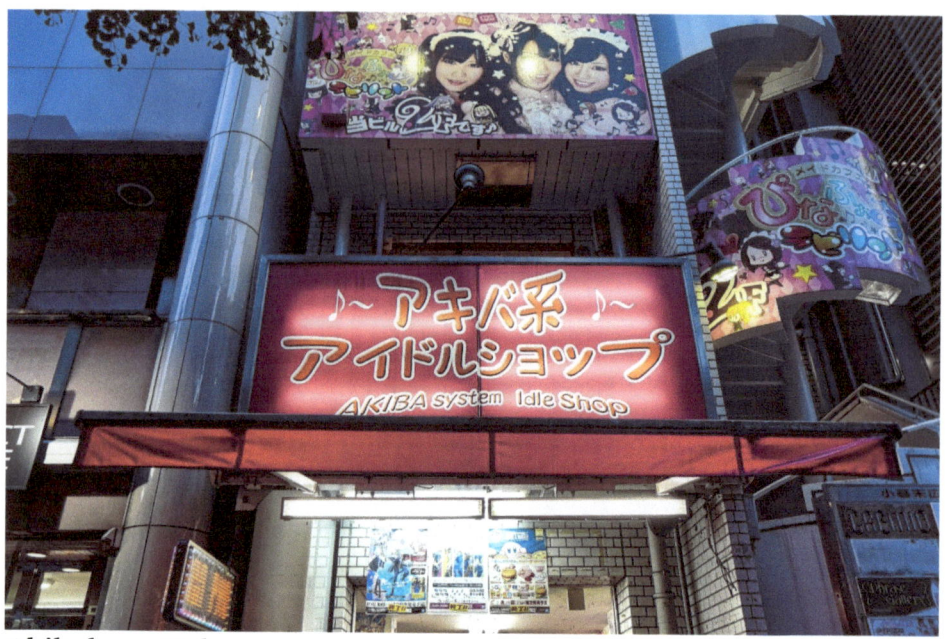

Akihabara, Tokyo

Description:

With its vibrant storefronts, Akihabara is a popular photo location.

AKIHABARA
STREET SIGNS

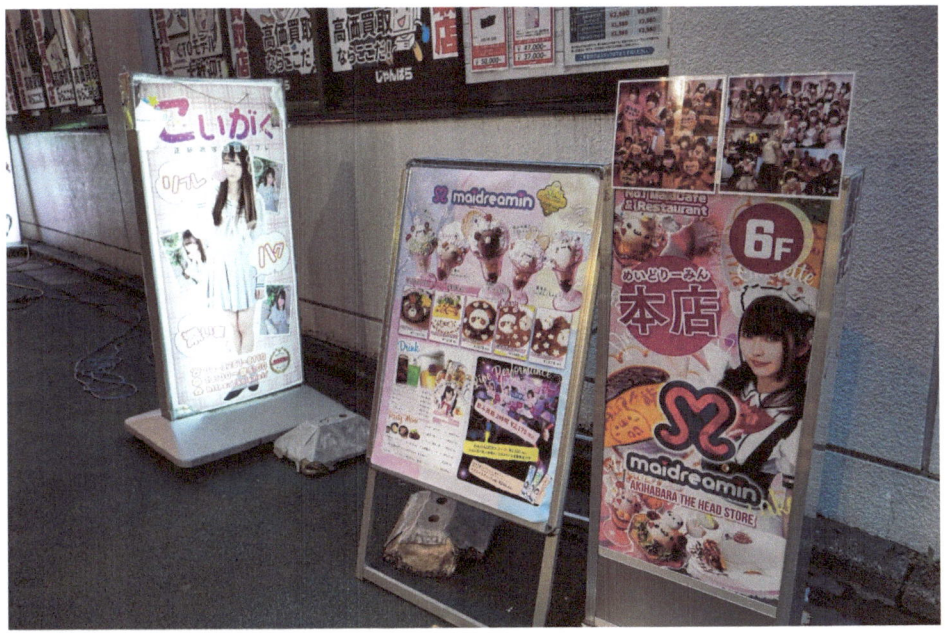

Akihabara, Tokyo

Description:

Subcultures thrive and are celebrated in this city.

AKIHABARA EVENING

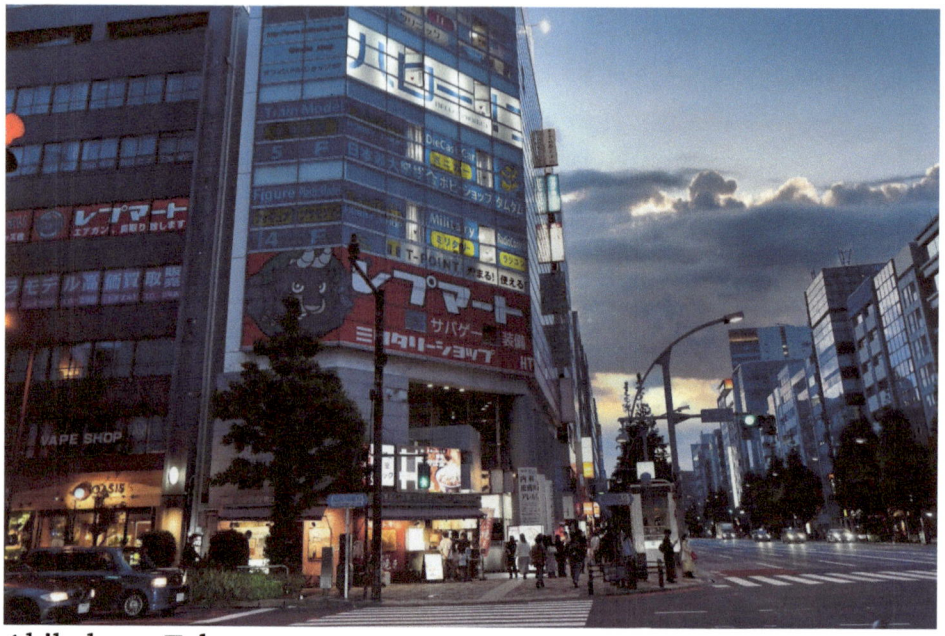

Akihabara, Tokyo

Description:

The station is well-connected to other popular Tokyo neighbor-hoods like Ueno and Asakusa.

AKIHABARA SUNSET

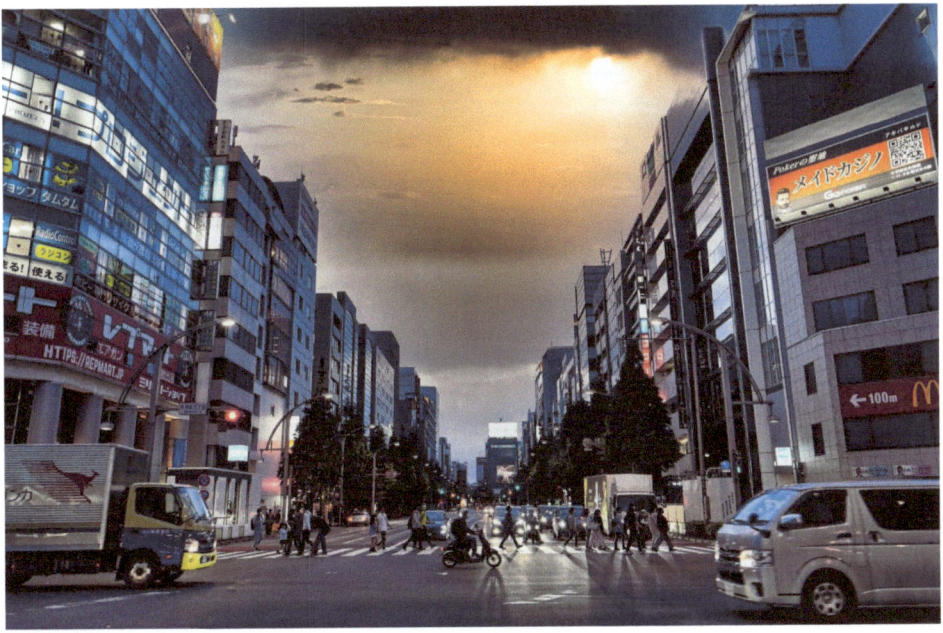

Akihabara, Tokyo

Description:

Annual events, conventions, and exhibitions are held in the district.

AKIHABARA NIGHT CROSSING

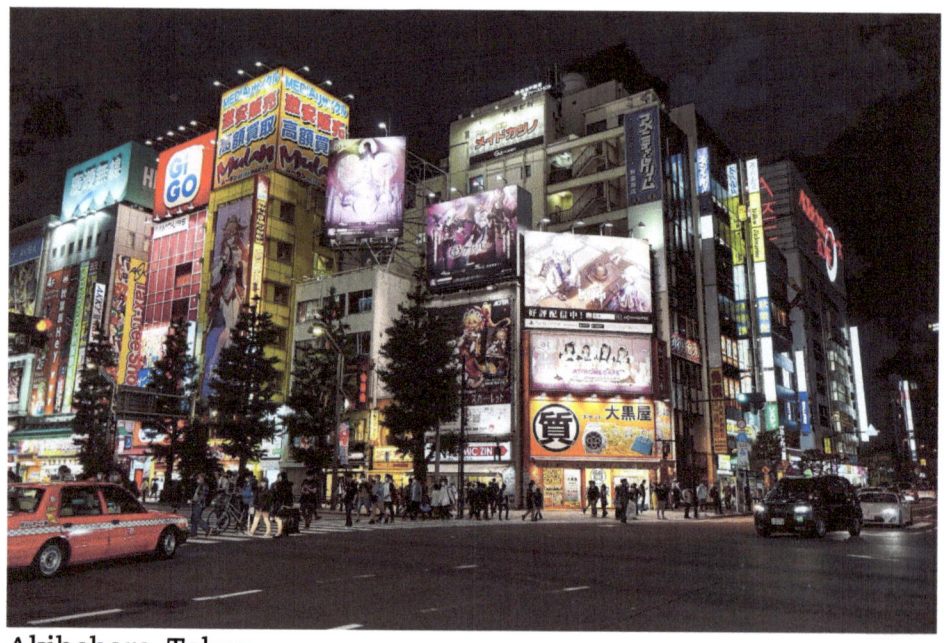

Akihabara, Tokyo

Description:

The streets surrounding the station are pedestrian-friendly, making it simple to explore on foot.

AKIHABARA TAXI CROSSING

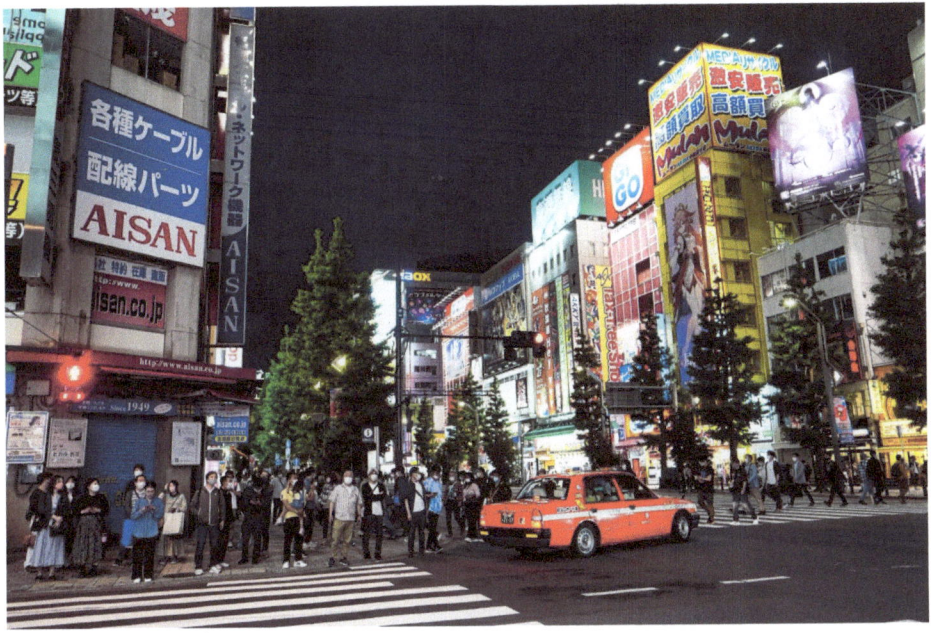

Akihabara, Tokyo

Description:

The vibrancy and energy of Akihabara are palpable, creating a one-of-a-kind atmosphere.

AKIHABARA BIC CAMERA NIGHT

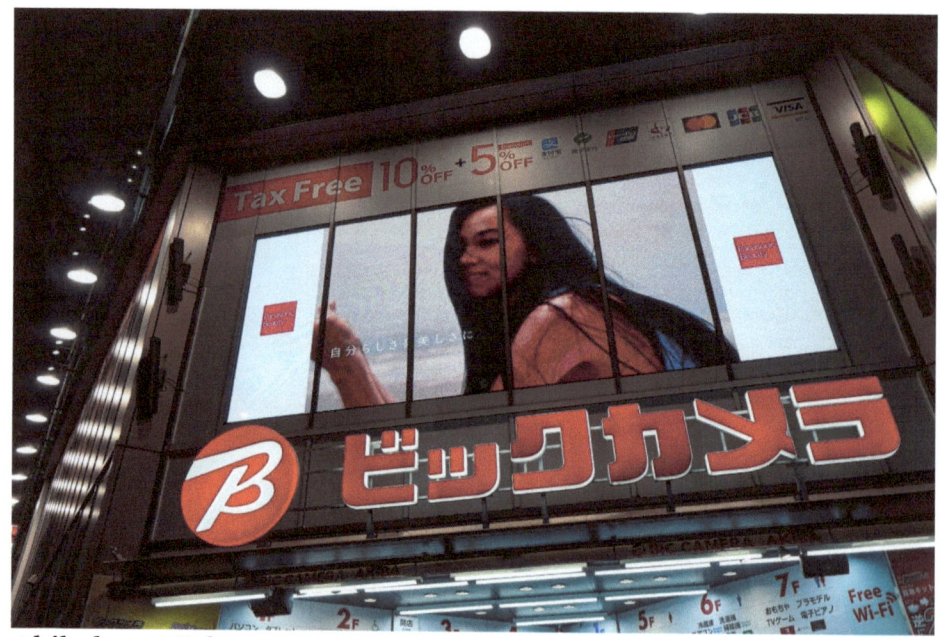

Akihabara, Tokyo

Description:

Exploring Akihabara is like entering a different world, one that embraces its pop culture wholeheartedly.

LAMMTARRA
AKIHABARA

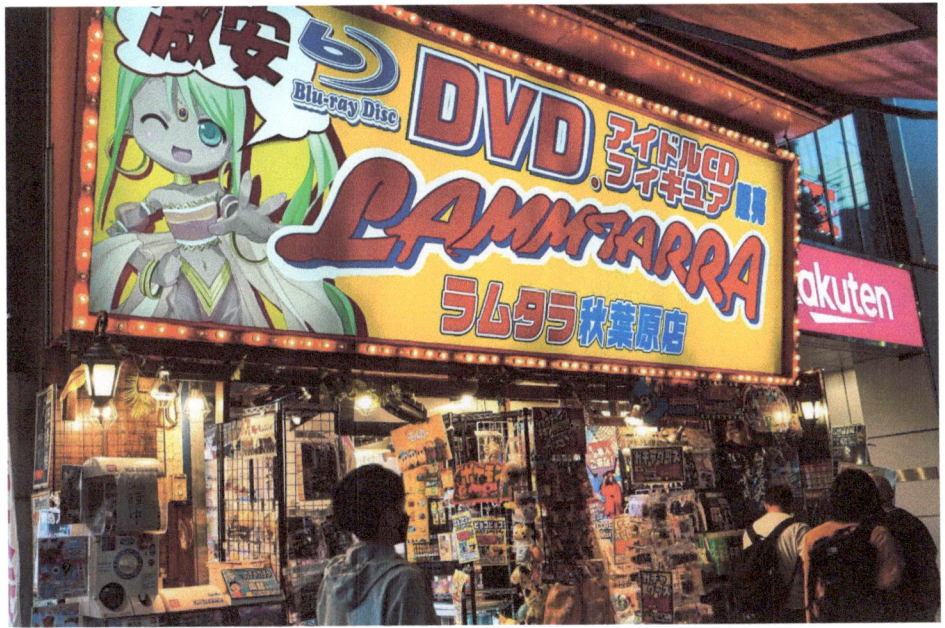

Akihabara, Tokyo

Description:

Visitors can also learn about the area's cultural history by visiting antique shops.

AKIHABARA GAME CENTER GAME PANIC

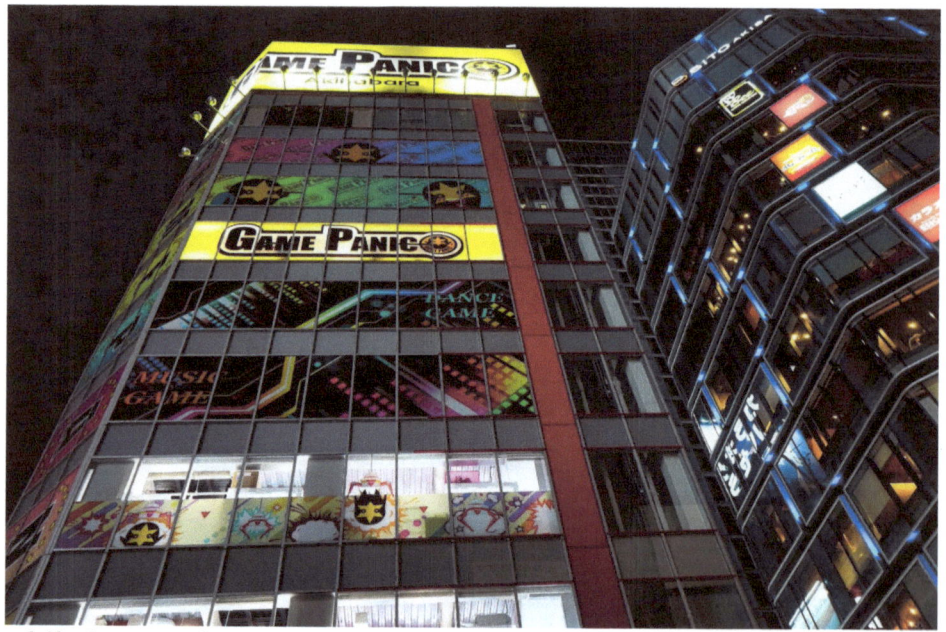

Akihabara, Tokyo

Description:

Akihabara fosters a sense of community among enthusiasts.

AKIHABARA
GAME PANIC

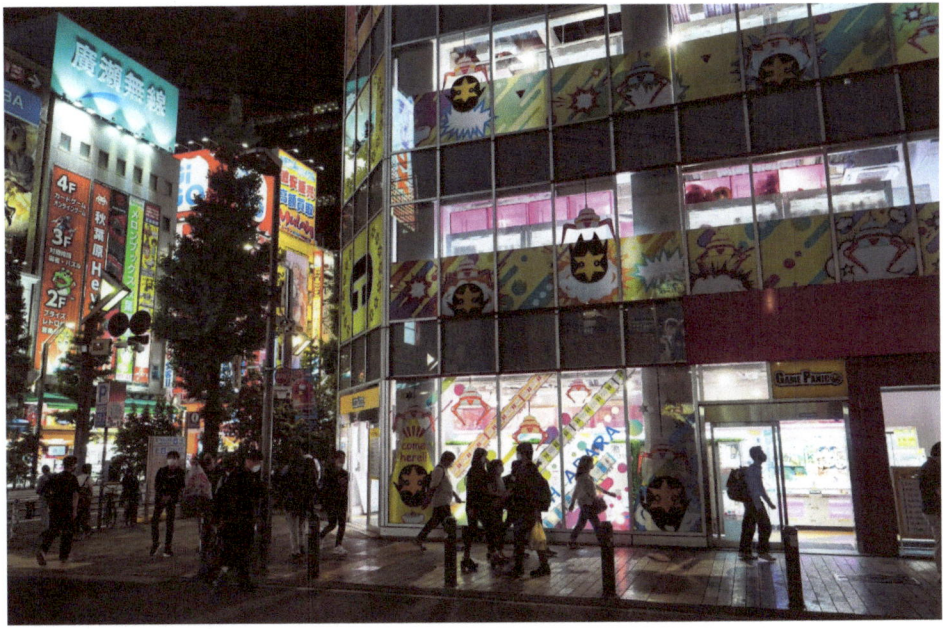

Akihabara, Tokyo

Description:

The area is a hotspot for pop idols, with concerts and events held on a regular basis.

AKIHABARA STATION (OUTSIDE)

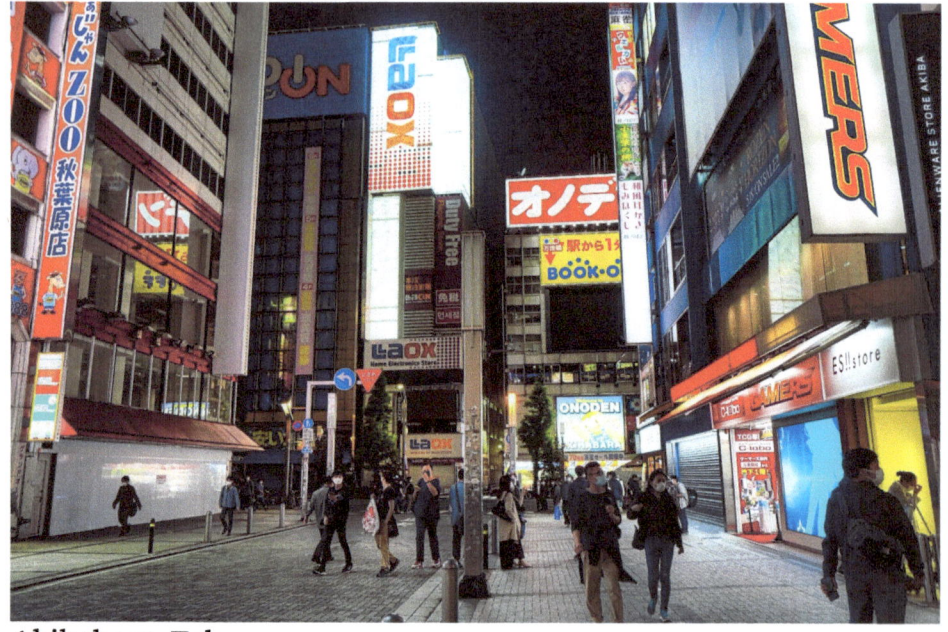

Akihabara, Tokyo

Description:

Akihabara Station is a cultural as well as a transportation hub.

AKIHABARA
STREET AD

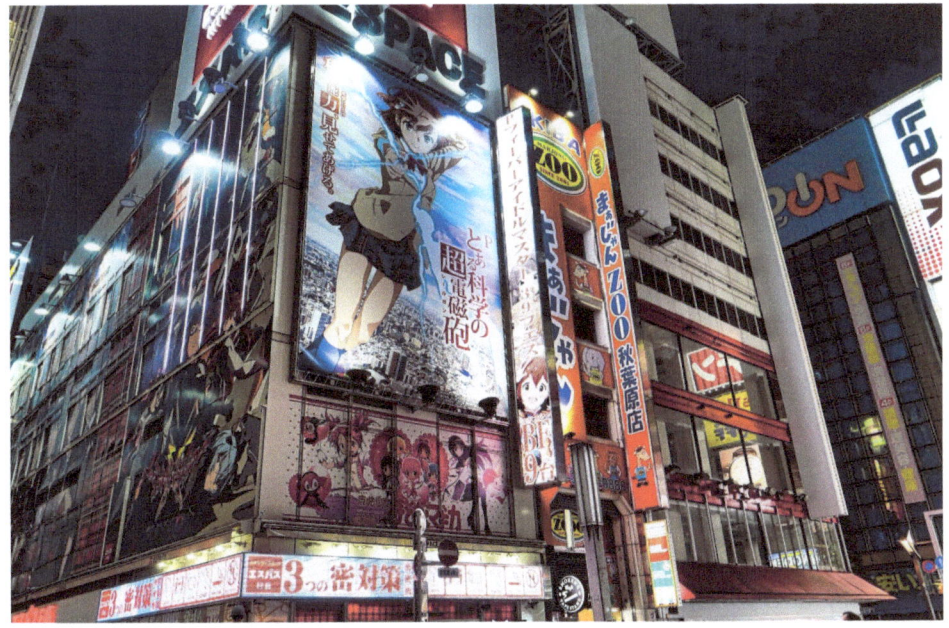

Akihabara, Tokyo

Description:

Akihabara is located in the Chiyoda ward, is a hub for visitors interested in both otaku culture and modern electronics.

AKIHABARA STREET POSTER

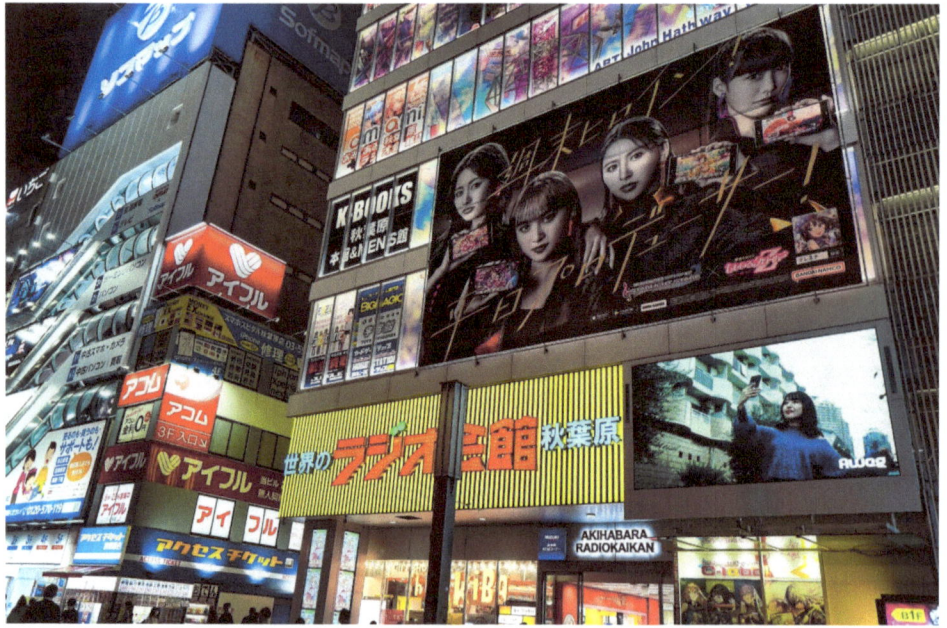

Akihabara, Tokyo

Description:

The area around Akihabara Station is synonymous with pop culture, providing fans with a glimpse into the worlds of anime, manga, and gaming.

AKIHABARA DOOR AD

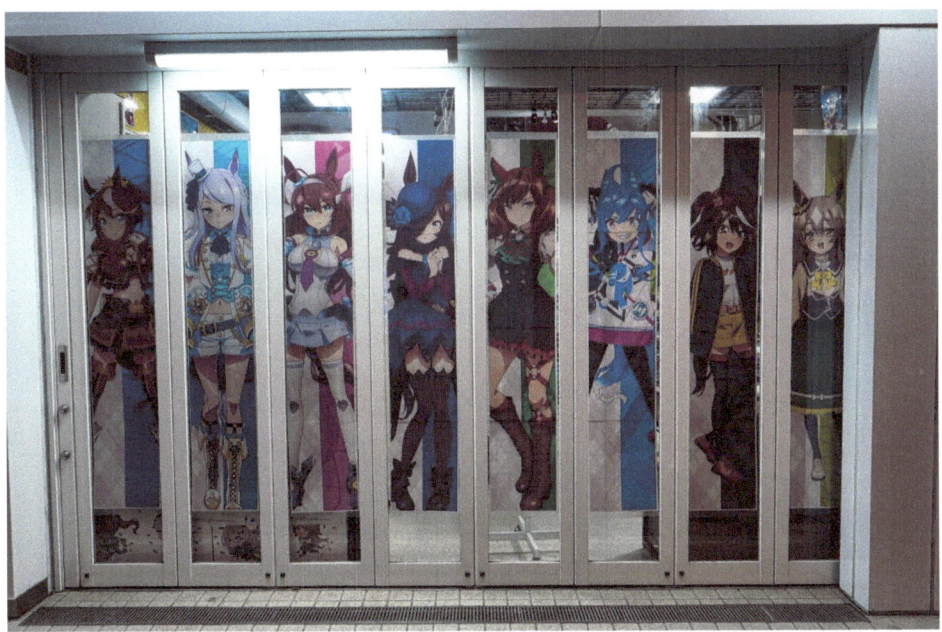

Akihabara, Tokyo

Description:

Navigating Akihabara Station can be an exciting experience because it provides access to a plethora of shops.

SHIBUYA CROSSING NIGHT

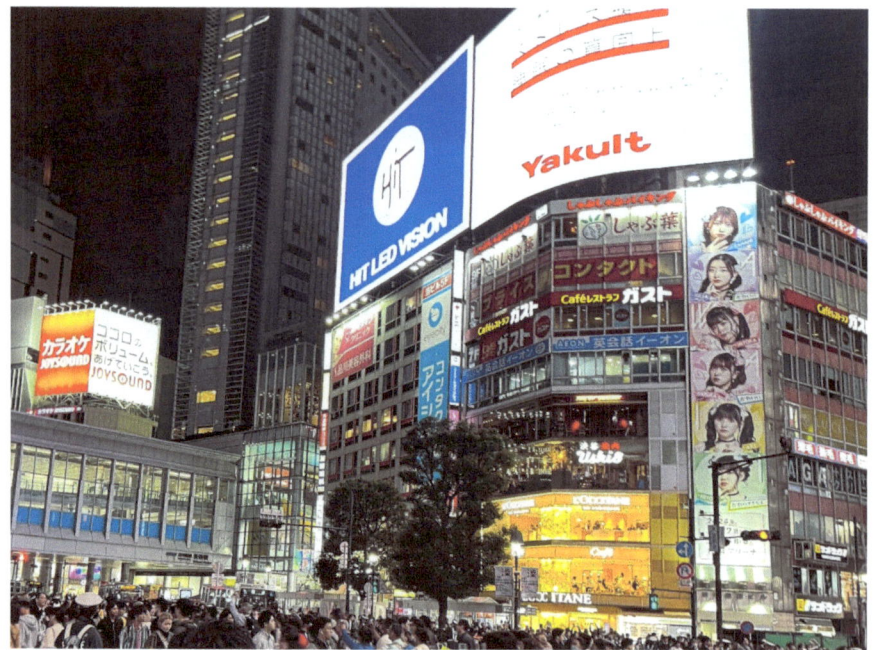

Shibuya, Tokyo

Description:

Shibuya, with its iconic Scramble Crossing, is a buzzing urban hub where thousands of people cross paths every day.

SHIBUYA CROSSING NIGHT

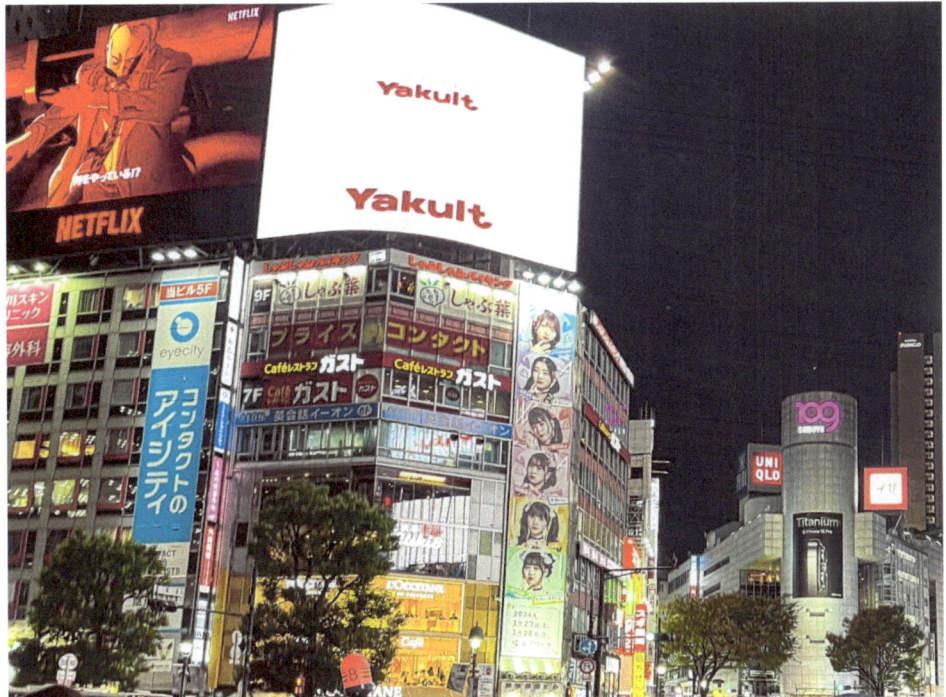

Shibuya, Tokyo

Description:
The neon-lit Shibuya district embodies Tokyo's vibrant nightlife and entertainment.

SHIBUYA CENTER STREET

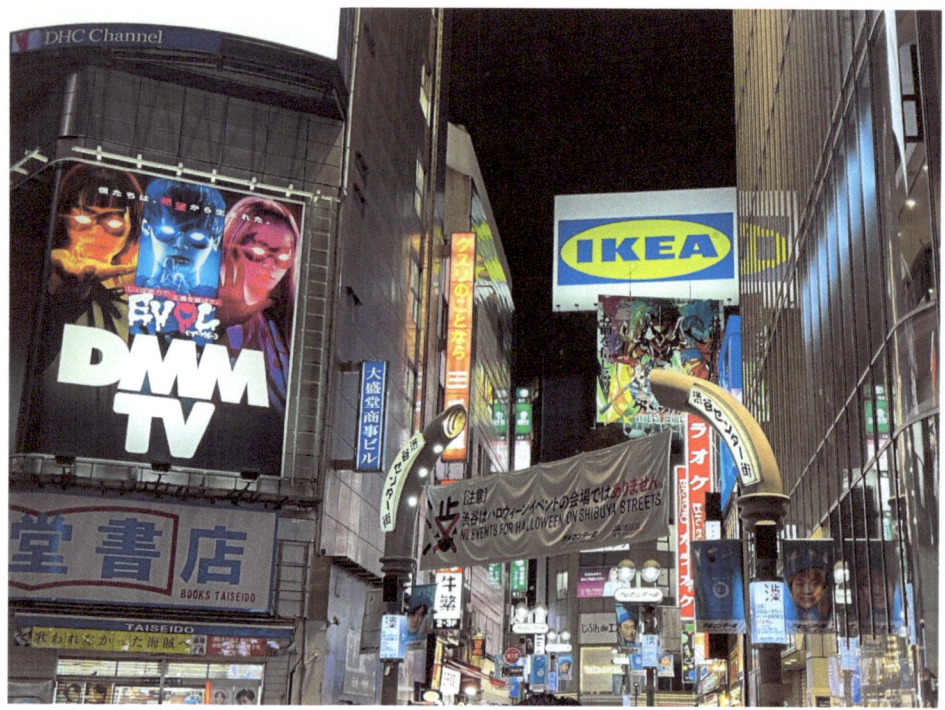

Shibuya, Tokyo

Description:

Shibuya Center Street, also known as "Center Gai," is a bustling pedestrian street lined with shops and restaurants.

SHIBUYA CENTER
STREET SIGNS

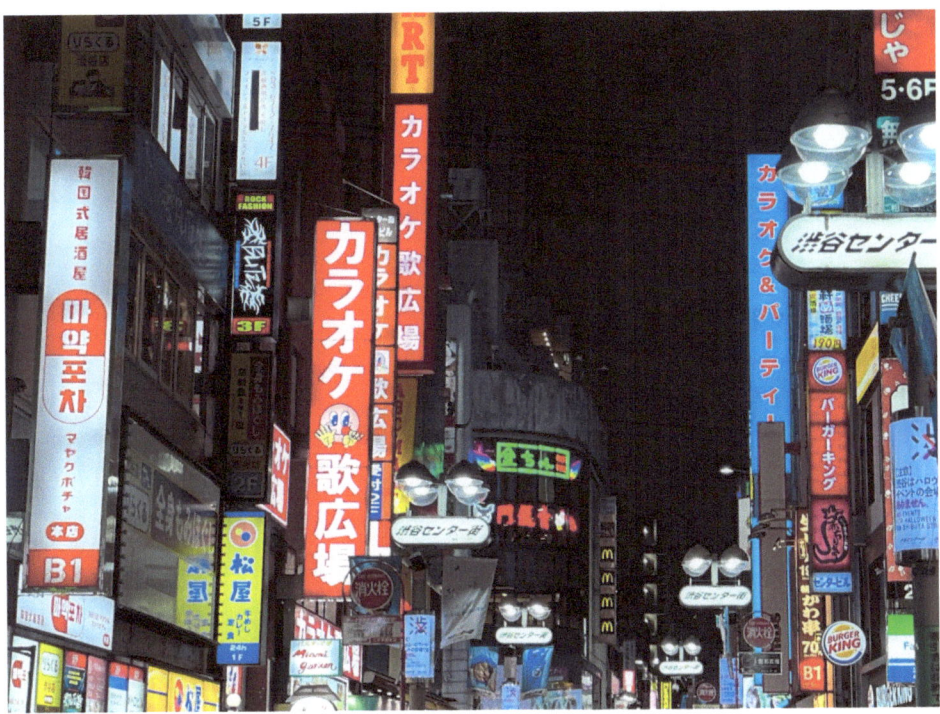

Shibuya, Tokyo

Description:

Shibuya's lights and illuminated billboards create a mesmerizing spectacle at night, capturing the energy of the city.

SHIBUYA 109 DEPARTMENT STORE

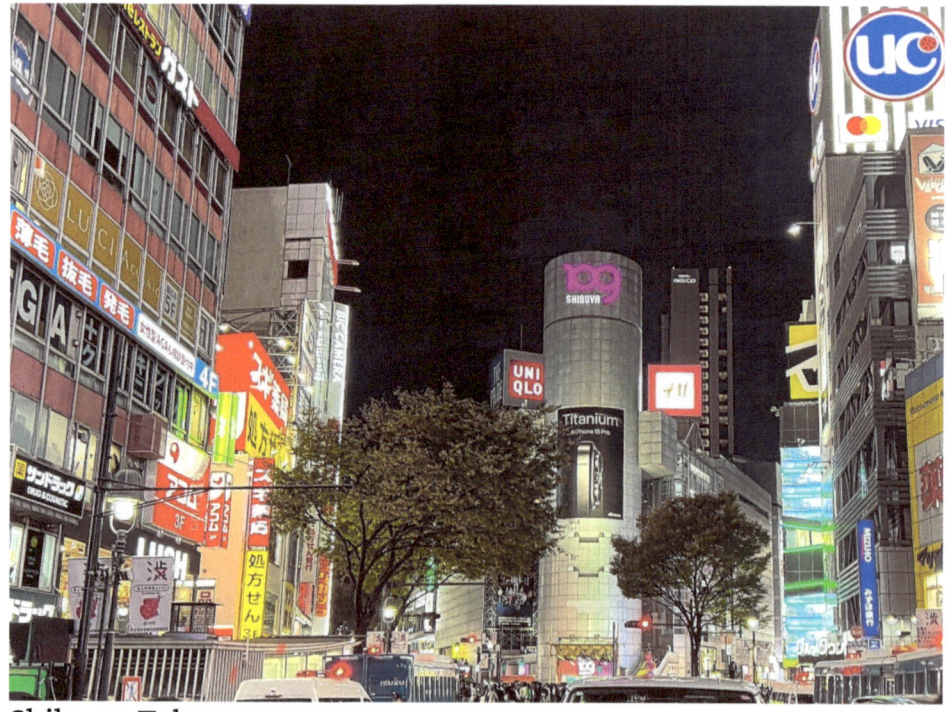

Shibuya, Tokyo

Description:

Shibuya's department stores, including Shibuya 109 and Shibuya Hikarie, provide an unparalleled shopping experience.

TOKYO PAUL'S
OTHER BOOKS

Title:
Japan Info Guide: Tips & Photos For An Amazing Experience in Japan!

Description:
This book is your ticket to the most current, relevant recommendations on what to see and skip and what undiscovered gems are waiting for you. I share my years of experience traveling and living in Japan with you. With your dependable travel buddy, see more than a hundred temples in Kyoto, unwind in a hot spring strewn over the island, and savor the diversity of Japan's delicious foods. Start your tour immediately, enjoy my high-quality photos, and get to the heart of Japan with me.

Book Cover:

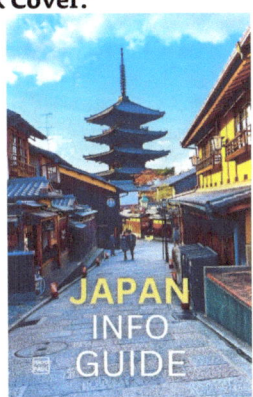

Tokyo Paul's Other Books

Title:
Japan Photobook 2023

Description:
This wonderful Japan Photobook contains
more than 75 pages of breathtaking images
from my YouTube Japan travels. You can visit
the same locations because they are well-
marked! Discover the gorgeous towns and
sites of Japan through breathtaking photo-
graphs. Let the stunning cityscapes, festival
scenes, cherry blossoms, and illuminations
take you there! This book includes images
of excellent quality and resolution. Every
city, including Akihabara, Asakusa, Yoko-
hama, Ueno, Ginza, Hakone, Nikko, etc., has
a breathtaking atmosphere. This fantastic
book beautifully captures Japan's incredible
energy and way of life.

Book Cover:

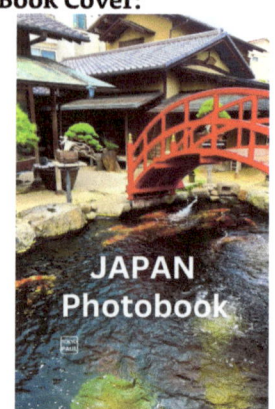

Tokyo Paul's Other Books

Title:	Book Cover:
Japan Photography Book 2023 Stunning Photos of Japanese Cityscapes, Shrines, Festivals & Nature	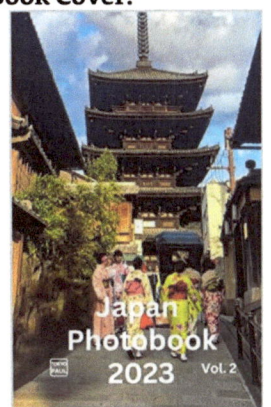
Description: Over 75 pages of NEW Stunning Pictures and Photos of Cityscapes, Shrines, Festivals & Nature in this fantastic Japan Photo Book from my YouTube Japan walks. This book is an affordable and cost-effective way to immerse yourself in Japan and see unique sights not seen anywhere else! Experience these breathtaking cities and sights of Japan through amazing photos and be transported to Japan via photos and images in the book; beautiful cityscapes, festival events, and cherry blossoms & illuminations!	

Tokyo Paul's Other Books

Title:
Japan and Its Famous Regional Foods &
Things

Description:
This comprehensive guidebook explores
Japan's rich culture and history through its
47 prefectures. From the bustling streets of
Tokyo to the tranquil landscapes of Okinawa,
discover each region's unique characteristics
and famous attractions. From the histor-
ical temples and shrines in Kyoto to the
renowned seafood of Hokkaido, this book
delves deep into the heart of Japan, detailing
the famous regional specialties, delicious
local cuisines, and traditional customs of
each prefecture. With detailed information,
this book is perfect for travelers planning
their next trip to Japan and those wanting to
deepen their understanding of Japan.

Book Cover:

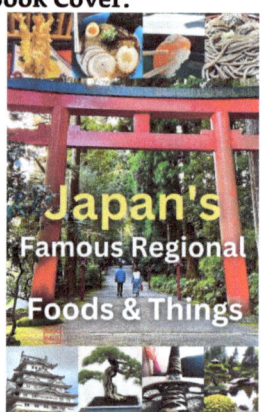

Tokyo Paul's Other Books

Title: Tokyo Info Guide: Tips & Photos For Traveling in Japan **Description:** This book is your best travel companion for discovering Tokyo's lively and diverse cityscape. This thorough guidebook offers in-depth details on the city's history, culture, prominent attractions, helpful advice for navigating the city like a local, and a map of the most popular train line. A valuable tool for first-time tourists, the guidebook also offers essential information on the Japanese language. The Tokyo Guidebook is the ideal travel companion for anyone visiting Tokyo, Japan.	**Book Cover:** 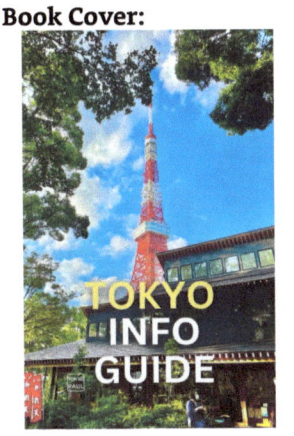

Tokyo Paul's Other Books

Title:
Japan Trip Planner (Journal) Kindle Edition

Description:
Compact Size: 6 inches by 9 inches
Ample space for writing notes for 10-15 plus trips
Included Sections:
• 100 Must-See Recommendations, 75 Places & 25 Seasonal Events by Popularity
• Budget Log Section
• Checklists: Pre-trip Checklist, Foods Checklist

Book Cover:

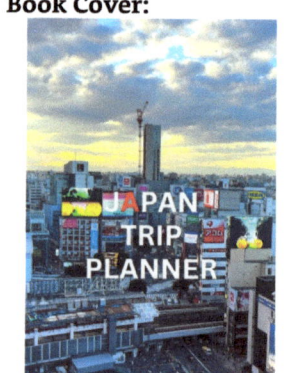

ABOUT THE AUTHOR

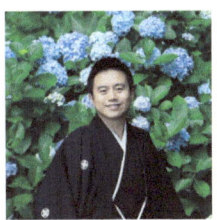

Tokyo Paul is an Asian American who has lived in Japan for over seven years. He's lived everywhere, from Osaka to Nagasaki to Toyama to Tokyo in Japan. He enjoys live-streaming videos on YouTube on his channel. He is an avid sushi fan and goes to his favorite sushi restaurant Sushiro every week. He is also on Twitter, Instagram, and Facebook if you wish to follow him for more information about Japan.

Thank you for finishing this book with me. I'm Tokyo Paul. Consider checking me out on YouTube, search Tokyo Paul to watch my videos about Japan, or any other social media platform such as Facebook, Instagram, and Twitter. Safe journeys, everyone!

The End

www.ingramcontent.com/pod-product-compliance
Lightning Source LLC
Chambersburg PA
CBHW050809290526
45792CB00001B/42